#FMJ

TRUST
TRANSITION
TRADE

Jane Gallina
AirplaneJane

#FMJ Trust Transition Trade
How Successful Traders Said It, Did It, and Lived It

Tellwell Talent
www.tellwell.ca

ISBN
978-1-77302-902-3 (Hardcover)
978-1-77302-887-3 (Paperback)
978-1-77302-888-0 (eBook)

Dedicated to my husband, Parham;
and to my two daughters,
Sienna Jane and Scarlett Victoria.

A portion of the profits will be donated to
The Make-A-Wish Foundation.

Acknowledgements

First, I would like to thank my husband for reminding me that trading is a passion of mine. Second, I would like to thank all my followers who made me want to share more and actually put this in writing. Thank you to @OutlierK, @randyvannoort, and my best friend Jan for their help in titling the book. Thank you to Jacob Whitish for all of his ideas and for interviewing me. And thank you to my family and friends who have supported me throughout this entire journey. This is just the beginning...

Table of Contents

Introduction

#FMJ What's that you say? I'm referring to the Forget My Job or F@%K My Job mentality I developed after giving birth to my first daughter in August of 2014. This shift in mentality came from a deep place in my mind and heart to provide for my newborn. I had a new sense of survival based on my drive to be available to my baby at home and to provide for her basic needs of shelter, food, and clothing. Your mind shifts into protection mode once you have a child, and mine said, "Find a job that gives you the ability to be at home, to be present for your child, and to still provide."

My husband reminded me about my value trading success in the past, and suggested that maybe I should return to investing. Trading was something I loved, but as a job from home, I wanted it to be something requiring everyday interactions instead of only once a month. As a value investor, I had spent time finding long term holdings to grow. Looking back, I now know that value investing over the long term tends to be skewed to grow in value. When you have big money investors that deal with retirement accounts and 401ks, they invest the money and park it in stocks in the form of a mutual fund or an annuity. Those continued investments grow the value of the stock over time.

In that sense, value investing works over the long term, but you are not going to see incredible returns. If you happen to be invested in a stock that gets bought out, you might see the stock jump an incredible amount overnight. You then have the choice to either hold onto it, or sell it and capitalize on the gains. After researching day trading online, I quickly discovered that daily gains of capital from 5% to 300% were possible. I was hooked!

In my desire to learn more about day trading, I found Timothy Sykes. When you Google 'How to learn day trading', Tim is found all over the internet! Timothy Sykes is known as a penny stock guru who took $12,415 of bar mitzvah money and turned into in $4 million dollars. After doing my due diligence researching both him and his tools, I found that students had success with his programs. His initial slogan "I want you to be my next millionaire student" resonated with me.

Throughout this thought process, as a female going after my goal I never thought that there would be any hurdles. I never questioned my capabilities as a female to achieve any goal. Instead, I continued on my journey and worked hard to get what I wanted.

I began studying hard with 'Tim's Challenge Program'. As I watched his videos, I was a sponge that absorbed all of the information provided. With the amount of information given, you need to stay consistent and study every day! In Tim's DVD *How to Make Millions*, he recommends that everyone open a Twitter account so as to have instantaneous access to stock information that people post. That's when **AirplaneJane** was born!

At that point I began scouring Twitter accounts to find other knowledgeable traders I could follow. I sought traders who offered regular posts of great information to learn from. From my analytics on Twitter, I found that 88% of my following was male. I was surprised by this percentage. In my mind, I felt this inequality was unjustified. In the meantime, I continued studying and working hard to find a strategy that worked for me. I was a good student and followed Tim's recommendations.

One of Tim's blog posts provides a list of recommended books about trading. From reading a couple of these books, I learned a lot. As you will see, these books are also recommended by the traders presented in this book. To me this proves that they are great educational tools for everyone. I first read *Market Wizards* by Jack Schwager and fell in love with the interview style of delving into the WHY behind each trader's success. I also appreciated that he asked about the pitfalls as well.

Hearing about the experiences of well-known day traders made me want to read another book in the same style. Coincidentally I saw a tweet from @InvestorsLive about the new release of *Momo Traders* by Brady Dahl in October 2015. This is a contemporary publication of day traders who are in tune with today's stock market. I was captivated. I thought this would be something I could do, and more importantly something I would want to do, as my career.

I continued to study hard and practice first with paper trading. Once I had established a strategy that built my confidence and consistency, I traded real money in my account. In learning from others and seeing their real time tweets, I thought I would share my entries and exits. I could help new traders in the same manner that I had learned from others.

I simply shared my experience on my Twitter account, and gradually people started asking me questions. Rather than limit my responses to a tweet, I started my blog entitled SEEJANETRADE. com, where I share weekly updates and answer questions that people email me. I know what it is like to be overwhelmed by all the terms and information at the beginning of your trading journey. In fact, I'm continually studying and learning every day.

Hearing about other traders' paths to success led me to try to find a book about women who have succeeded in trading. I combed the internet to find what I was looking for in a book. While I found individual books written by women about trading, I could not find any compilations of trading biographies. So that is why I have created this book about women traders.

After searching all corners of the globe, I found seven other women willing to describe their diverse roads toward a career in trading. What I have found to be different about women is our nurturing and sharing attitudes. There are women traders out there, but many have not gone public. Many women traders are conservative, risk adverse, and base their approach of helping others.

All of the women in this book trade with a passion. They have experience ranging from five months to over 20 years. Some traders started as professionals, and some started from their phones. The diversity is amazing, and the uniqueness lies in how each trader holds their own fingerprint trading style.

In order to succeed with your goals you need to master yourself. You need to see your weaknesses and your strengths. Your true self will be reflected in your trades. If you are a person who has a hard time cutting unhealthy relationships from your life, then you will probably have a hard time cutting losers. On the other hand, if you have a hard time making decisions, then you might start off watching the market and be too scared to enter for fear that you will make the wrong move. Trading will challenge you to really face your fears and your weaknesses. When you take the time to analyze your trades and the related emotions, then you will see your bottom line improve. Trading has its ups and downs. As long as you keep the gains bigger than the losses, you will grow not only yourself but also your account.

There is no limitation in your future except for the hurdles that you put in your mind. When you put forth daily effort towards your goal of creating a better life for yourself, you will gradually achieve that goal. Before you know it, you will find that you are living the life you had once only dreamed about. Never did I think I would be a trader or a writer, but my goal of sharing and improving others' lives made it happen.

If you are new to AirplaneJane and myself, please know that I will always try to encourage and inspire you to be the best version of yourself. In order to achieve your potential, you need to keep a positive mindset. You will see that the women interviewed in this book have a passion to be traders, and they have followed their passion through to make it happen. They have shared their perspectives, tips, and tools for you to succeed as well.

This is just the beginning of your success story.

Ashley Mcrae

USA

Twitter: @jinx180

Ashley began following me on Twitter when I was taking my first steps to create this book. As we began chatting about our trading experiences, I quickly learned that Ashley is a mother of two and a nurse with a new passion for day trading. Like mine, her passion was unleashed while she was on maternity leave with her son.

Jane: You're down in Texas, correct?

Ashley: Yes, I'm in Texas.

Jane: How did trading come into your life?

Ashley: I started getting into it while I was on maternity leave. I was on social media a lot because I was breastfeeding all the time. One of my friends posted something like, "Netflix went up 17%. Tomorrow, I'm going to be a shareholder." I looked into it, and it was about $117. I thought, "That's a lot of money." It started going down, and that's when I started watching the tickers. I'm not really sure why I started doing that, but I did.

In that thread, someone said, "No, you need to watch Leapfrog. They're going to be bought out by VTech, and it's going to be a good buy. Invest, invest, invest." I started looking up things about the stock market, but it was all in another language that I just couldn't understand. I started researching a lot and trying to learn it. I felt that if I'm capable of learning nursing stuff, then I can surely figure this out. I did lot of Googling, a lot of research, and eventually I ended up just getting an app on my phone: Robinhood. With that, I was able to look at a bunch of tickers.

I looked at Leapfrog, and I said, okay, I'm going to play with this a little bit. I think this was around Christmas time, and I put $200 into my Robinhood account and I bought a little over a couple hundred shares of Leapfrog. At the time, Leapfrog was around 64 cents. I held it; nothing happened. I just held it.

Then one day, the news of a contract with VTech came out . It went up to close 96 cents, and so then I started doing the math. If I had put $3000 into this and it had jumped like that ... This is really something. I started Googling more about where I could learn about this, and eventually I came across Tim Sykes. He kept coming up on a bunch of searches.

I looked into a lot of people, but he was the one who kept coming up. His website was pretty neat, but I was thinking, this guy is really good at marketing. He's just trying to sell me something. I started looking at his YouTube videos. He had a book, *An American Hedge Fund*, and I ordered it on Amazon. That really helped me get into his headspace to see how he got into it.

I signed up for Tim Alerts and the chatroom. Then I decided, you know what? I have saved up quite a bit of money for maternity leave and I'm just going to put $2000 into my account and I'm going to try this. I'm going to see how it goes. I started trading mostly from alerts from the chatroom, and honestly it was just dumb luck.

Everything I was investing in I was giving it all or nothing. It was all hitting. I'd make $60 and then like $100, and then ... My biggest one was...$900 in one day. Then I started losing money, because I had no strategy. I said ok, I'm going to stop, take a look at what I'm doing.

I went from Tim Alerts to the Silver Subscription and started watching all of Tim's videos and things. I started trying to teach myself technical analysis and looking at the charts. That's pretty much how I got into it: I just threw myself into it out of boredom.

Jane: Great, so would you say that Tim is pretty much your mentor with day trading?

Ashley: Yes, definitely. He was the main one I looked at and then I started following you.

Jane: Thank you.

Ashley: And reading your blog, and you were like me. You were on maternity leave too. I followed some of your updates. The stocks you follow are generally a little bit pricier than penny stocks, so I try to stay with the lower priced stocks. It is interesting to me, the different strategies.

Jane: Definitely. That's something that I learned from Tim. As well, his goal is to make traders become self-sufficient with their own strategies so that you learn from him, and then you move forward into your own strategy. Have you found anything that works for you, like a particular strategy that you're comfortable with, or that you've sort of evolved into after your time studying? When did you start? ... Was it back in January? So you've been doing it now just about five months?

Ashley: Yeah... I think my first trade was in January 2016, and then I held that trade for a while. I think February is when I started trading more regularly.

Jane: Do you have any sort of strategy or setup that you look at in going forward? For me I tend to look for reversal bounces.

Ashley: Right. I'm still trying to figure that out. I've tried a lot of different strategies. I've tried gap trading, started looking at them. Tried that. Sometimes I've been okay with it. I've tried reversals, I've tried breakouts. Mostly what I do is I look for something with news. I go and see what has been gaining the day before, what's newsworthy.

           I like earnings because I can read them. This month I was going to start trying to work on shorting. I haven't shorted anything yet, and I know that's something I really need to at least try out, and so my next goal is to learn how to short sell.

Jane: What do you typically do for your trading day setup? Do you get up, have a cup of coffee? Do you look at news for the day?

Ashley: I try to have a watch list the night before, but with my son, sometimes I'm not able to leave him and go research. Generally in the morning I get up. My day starts with my older son. He goes to school so I'll get up with him, and that's about 5:30 Central Time. It's 6:30 Eastern Time. I'll have a cup of coffee and something to eat.

Then I just start going through the news. Yahoo Finance, I look at what's gapping. I get into chatrooms, see what people are bringing up for news articles, and I create my watch list and see what I'm going to do. I get on E-Trade Pro, start running my scanner, and then just see what happens for the day.

Jane: Very nice. Have you transitioned from Robinhood into E-Trade?

Ashley: Yeah. I had Robinhood because it was easy. It was an app on my phone and I really liked it, but after I started trading more, I realized that it wasn't the best broker. I couldn't call after hours. Not all trades are available. You can't short sell, and so I opened one with E-Trade.

With the Pattern Day Trader rule, you can only do three rolling trades a week. I thought if I had two brokers, then I could make six trades a week. Eventually I opened up an E-Trade account, and I use both of those.

Jane: Are there any indicators that you use for your style of trading? You look at the news particularly, and you say you're looking more at technical analysis as well, correct?

Ashley: Right. I try to. I would be successful if I stuck to that strategy to check the chart and news. Usually though I get very emotional while trading and seeing alerts in a chatroom. I see alerts of tickers starting to go up and I just want to get in on it.

Sometimes I will just jump in if I think something's breaking out. You don't have much time to think about it, which is my problem, and I end up trading emotionally. That's one of those rules. I try to contain myself.

Jane: When you're trading, do you typically scale in and out of trades, or do you just go all in like you said at the beginning when you first started, or do you size accordingly to risk-reward?

Ashley: It depends. Sometimes I'll go all in if I'm really confident. I haven't done that in a long time since I started. I had a really bad month where I was losing, and so after that, I brought it down. I said to myself, "I'm going to start trying different setups." I had a rule where I was going to do 100 shares just to learn. I was going to do 100 shares and that was it. That way if it went bad, it wasn't that horribly bad. If it went well, it was a good learning experience and I would make a little bit of money. Now I kind of portion myself out. It just really depends on what I have to work with, what my last trade was. Usually I cut my account in half. It just depends. It's usually about half, and then I'll just take a nice, round number and trade that.

Jane: Do you add to your losers or your winners at all, or do you just trade 50% of your account? How do you typically strategize?

Ashley: Sometimes I will add if I'm losing, and I will keep adding. I've gotten into trouble with that, so I just play it case by case. Sometimes it helps me out. That was actually something I just recently started doing, and I'm still not sure how I feel about it. I had a couple of bad trades last week. Neither of them worked out too well, and I held both of them just too long. That was another learning experience. Every time I fail, I make a new rule: don't do this again. I'm not sure how I feel about that yet. I think it could work for my benefit; it just hasn't quite yet.

Jane: I understand completely. You're saying you're developing your rules as you go. Do you have any sort of hard-set rules that you've already developed?

Ashley: I have some. I can't say that I've followed them very well, but one of them is to cut losses quickly. If it goes under this, I'm out. I almost never do that though. That's something I'm trying to get better at: you know, just get out. It's hard for me because I feel like I'm losing my trade. The money's going to have to balance or it's going to have to go back through, and so I'm not going to be able to trade with this again for three days.

That's a mindset I just have to get over and I'm still working on it. When I sell a trade that's going badly, if I would've just waited just a little bit longer and given it more time, then it would have done what I thought it was going to do. I just need to cut losses quickly, but it's hard. I'm still having trouble with that, but that is a rule I'm trying to really, really stick to.

Other rules are not to hold onto my trades longer than 48 hours, because it's just not worked out well for me. I think holding overnight is beneficial, especially if they're going to gap in the morning, or within a short squeeze. I sometimes fall in love with a trade that keeps going up, and it's hard for me to let it go. Another challenge for me is to let the trade develop.

Sometimes I get out way too soon and I should've just given it more time and watched it. I started using level 2 now instead of watching to see when to get out. I say this is my goal, let me get out, when I really should have just let it continue to develop. I've lost a lot of profits that way too.

Jane: Before you go into a trade, do you do any sort of risk management, for example if it looks like it could go down 5 cents, but the potential is 20 cents on the upside, so it looks like a good trade?

Ashley: Yeah. I definitely set up parameters. Those, I'm pretty good at following. I'll say it can go down this, try and get in between here and here. It's usually 5 to 10 cents, depending on how much the trade is, and then I try to give it a scale of when to get out.

Jane: Now that you've gotten into it, you're say five months into it, do you find that you have more confidence in your trades, and you're able to have assurance when you get into a trade?

Ashley: I do and I don't. I feel more confident, but I know what I'm doing a little bit more. I definitely know way more than I did when I first started, but I was just throwing my trades out when I first started. Now I'm much more cautious, and I think the more I've learned, the more scared I have become. The more hesitant. I think I can do this. I don't know. It's weird. I enjoy it, but I'm worried about how it can go.

Jane: Right now you have your six trades a week. How many trades would you say you usually do in a day? Would you say that it's more emotionally-based, where you're going to trade two a day because that looks like a great trading day? How do you delegate your six trades?

Ashley: Another rule I made was not to do more than two trades a day. I feel that at my current level, I'm not able to watch them both, or watch too many. I'm making mistakes and I'm not executing them to the best of my ability. I'm trying to stay under two trades, or ideally just one trade a day if I can.

Today I didn't trade. I'm waiting for money to go in. I made a bunch of trades on Thursday and Friday that I had held almost all week, and so I'm waiting for my money to come back. Tomorrow I should be able to trade. I'm also trying to wait for setups to come to me instead of just wanting to trade. Right now, I'm starting on a smaller account, and there's definitely hurdles starting with a smaller account. I'm trying to wait for good trades and not waste my trades on just anything.

Jane: Do you think that having to wait for those trades with the pattern day trader rule makes you be more specific in selecting just the choice trades so that you can get in on the good ones? Or do you feel like it's just really difficult to learn because you're limited to say six trades a week? Basically do you feel the PDT rule is a positive or negative?

Ashley: Yeah, I think that having a day trader rule is pretty negative, honestly. I try to wait for good setups, but sometimes it's hard. What you think is a good setup could not be, and then you waste a trade. Whereas when you don't have the restriction you could just say, okay, that's a trade, I'll try another one. You can't do that with this rule, and that really hinders your learning experience.

Jane: You were saying you had a really rough month. Was it February when you were losing a lot? How did you recover from that? What was your biggest loss, and how did you recover from it?

Ashley: I think my biggest loss was almost $400.

Jane: Which is what in relation to your account?

Ashley: I had gained quite a bit, and then I started losing. It was maybe a sixth of my account at that point in time. It hurt, though. It was a painful trade, and I could've gotten out of it at so many points. I just kept thinking it couldn't possibly go lower. This was the bottom.

It was not. I kept thinking I would make it up; it would go up just a little bit more and then I would sell it, or it would bounce up. Just give me one more bounce and then I would sell it - but it just never did. It just kept sinking, and then of course I sold it, and the next morning it jumped right back up.

I had made a bunch of perilous trades. I was trying a bunch of different strategies, and I had done a lot of research. They weren't stupid trades on my part. I went in with a thesis; it's just that none of them worked out. The results were pretty battering on my confidence, and after that, I took a break. I said, okay, I'm not going to trade for a week. I'm going to watch the market; I'm going to paper trade and just really look at what I'm doing. The next week I came back and I think I still kept losing, but then I started thinking I'd have a good trade, then I'd have a bad trade, then I'd have a good trade. It just kind of kept going like that.

I have finally gotten to a point where I'm able to almost cut losses when I should cut losses, so that when I do have a bad trade, it's not really detrimental to me.

Jane: On the flip-side, what was your greatest trade so far? Do you remember the ticker?

Ashley: I think it was LIME, and I bought it ... It was breaking out, and...I was in that trade almost all day long. I bought it right at the market open, and it went down. I started losing, and then I had lost a couple hundred. I was like no, I'm going to hold onto it, and then it just started going up and up and up.

At one point I had made over...$1300. At this point in time, I think my biggest trade was $200. I was just ecstatic, and then it started going back down and I kept saying, oh I should have sold it when it was up here. I eventually sold it. I made about $900. That has still been my biggest trade.

Jane: What was that on the amount of investment that you put in? What was the return on your investment? Do you remember?

Ashley: I think it was about $2,800. At $1,400, the profit would have been 50%. When I ended up selling it, I only made about 30%. I would have made 50 to 60%, but I ended up profiting 30 to 40%.

Jane: For me, one of the most difficult things around the beginning was what I call "a deer in headlights". I would just watch the stock go up, and then I would watch it come back down, and I wouldn't lock in profits, and then I wouldn't cut the trade. I would ask myself, "What am I doing? I need to just pull the trigger on one way or the other."

Ashley: Yeah, I do that quite often still.

Jane: Now you use chatrooms. What tools are you using in your trading? Are you using Warrior Trading, Tim Sykes?

Ashley: Yeah, I use Tim a lot. I don't follow his trades because I've never won on his trades. Not because they haven't been good trades, but you get in after he does and then I ended up staying in after he got out. It never worked out for me. You don't really have time. When he makes a trade and you get that alert, you don't have time to look at it and go through everything, because by then it's already moved 5, 10 cents.

I quickly learned not to follow other people's trades, but I do look at his watch lists. A lot of times, they're similar to mine, which is great for confidence-building. I do use the chatroom. A lot of the people in there have great links they post. They put up a lot of amazing links. I use Twitter a lot to just follow leads.

I have scanners on my E-Trade. I have a phone app that I use at night where I put in a bunch of presets. I use that when I'm in bed with the baby. If I can't research, I get on there so I have an idea of what to do in the morning. Then I do the free chatroom with Warrior Trading on Mondays, and I also look at his list pretty much every morning after 8:00 am when he posts what his gap scanners do. That's all the stuff I use.

Jane: What would you say were your biggest hurdles of getting into trading? Any mental hurdles or fears, anything like that?

Ashley: I think the biggest fear was that I was doing something that was crazy. I didn't tell many people I was doing this because anyone I told would say you have no idea what you're doing. I felt that maybe I didn't, but then again I have researched this so much. For anyone who's tried to tell me anything about it, I think I know more about the stock market than they do at this point.

It's hard to explain to people, I guess. I have felt almost like they are thinking, well, you're a woman. I hate to say that, but I almost feel like I'm not taken seriously because of that. It's like they wonder, what could you possibly know about the stock market?

The day trading rule, that's been a hurdle. My Robinhood account has been a little bit of a hurdle for me, just because I can't do as much with it.

Then there's also the reality that I'm a mom, and my baby is still very much attached to me. I try to sit and watch, but sometimes I've got to go change a diaper and I'm in a trade, or he's screaming and I'm in a trade. That's definitely been a little bit of a barrier.

It's getting easier as he gets older, but that's definitely been something that's been hard.

Jane: What inspired you? You said it was your friend who told you about Netflix, right? That really inspired you to get into it. Was it just that you started researching and it just snowballed from there, or, maybe you could really do this as a way to make money?

Ashley: I had always been interested in the stock market. My dad would always talk about it. My dad was more of a 401k, long term investment guy, and so he always had big reactions when the stock market would go up or down. I had always believed that I needed a 401k, and I needed to invest in the stock market for retirement. As a nurse, I've always had a 401k, but it was always a portfolio put together by other people.

I didn't really know what was going on with my 401k, and I always felt like, if I was going to invest money in my retirement, this is probably something I need to learn about. This is my money. I should know what's going on with it. My friend had posted that about Netflix, and then when I saw what happened with Leapfrog, I realized that there's money to be made here - and it's not in the long term investing where you can make 20% a year on a good year. There are days I'm making 30 to 40% in a day. That's where the money's at! As I started making money, I just started thinking, how else could I be making money like this? This is almost unreal. I'm at home, I'm researching stuff but I'm at home, I'm taking care of my baby and I'm making more money than I would as a registered nurse. As an RN, I already make pretty good money, but it's a set amount. Your ambition only takes you so far.

With this you can go as far as you want. There are not very many ways to make money like this. There are not many opportunities like this. It's just an amazing opportunity, and honestly, I was trying to think, do I know anyone who does this? I don't. I wish I did sometimes, someone to talk to and move ideas around, but I don't know anyone who does this, especially not a woman.

I know long term investors who have stocks, but no one who does this day trading. I don't know why more people don't talk about it or do it.

Jane: That's what the goal of this book is, to try to open women's eyes so they can see that they can do it themselves.

Do you feel like reading medical charts or reading patterns, like heartbeats or anything like that with being a nurse, has helped you in reading the stock charts?

Ashley: That's interesting, because when I do look at the stock tickers, sometimes I think I'm looking at an EKG trace. I think that the data and the mindset of study are similar. If you can learn something, you can really learn anything. I think if you have that mindset to learn something, then the stock market isn't that hard to learn.

At first, I honestly thought it all looked like smoke and mirrors. My E-Trade Pro, if I pull that up right now, all my different windows seemed like they were in Chinese to me before. Now I know what every little thing means on there. It just takes time, and it's so intimidating, I think, but slowly you learn it. You can really benefit from it.

Jane: You're five months in, and so you've learned a lot - it's no longer Greek. As someone who's newer into it, what would you say to a woman who's just starting or just thinking about starting with day trading?

Ashley: I would say find a mentor, do a lot of research and study, and start by paper trading. I wish I would've done that.

Jane: Me too. Everybody told me that, but unfortunately I didn't listen. How have you handled your emotions in trading? Have you seen a development from when you first began to now, like you're not as anxious, you understand what's going on?

Ashley: Yeah, I still get really emotional. That's still something I'm working on. I honestly don't know if I'm ever going to not be emotional doing it, but I'm not as upset when a trade doesn't go well. I just realize that I made a mistake. If I made a really stupid mistake, like something I know I shouldn't have done, then I kind of look at it as, you knew this could happen, you went in anyway, and you need to learn from this now or never do it again.

The stock market's going to teach you. You can learn from it or keep losing money, so I tend to try and take it in stride now. Every loss I've had has been for a specific reason and I have a lot of lists. I have a long list now of what not to do. That's good for me, I think.

Jane: That's a very good way to look at it, where you're learning from an error instead of just ignoring it and then blowing up your account.

Ashley: Right.

Jane: How have you found balancing trading with being a mom? What are the positives and negatives for you?

Ashley: The positive is that at first I only had 12 weeks maternity leave but I've been able to be off for seven months now. I was not ready to give my baby up. I was not ready to leave him, and so to be able to be at home with him has been great. I'm not just sitting at home not doing anything. I feel like I'm contributing. My mind is active. I'm researching, I'm learning. I'm not just sitting at home going brain dead, which is kind of how I felt with my first son. That's been great. I have my iPhone, so if we go to the store, in every aisle I'm pulling up my stocks, I'm looking at them. If I'm holding anything or if I'm just watching, I'm completely addicted to watching the stock market now. I watch it almost every day. Even if I'm not in a trade, I'm watching something. We'll be out on the swing set, and I can have my phone right there. It's just very accessible, and I'm still present.

Jane: You mentioned having your phone out, like when you're grocery shopping and that sort of stuff. Do you find that you trade just specifically the 9:30 to 4:00 hours, or you do pre-market and after-hour trading as well?

Ashley: I have not really done much pre-market or aftermarket trading. Actually I haven't really done it at all. I've sold something after market because I was terrified, so I called them and sold it. That's one thing I would like to start doing. I just haven't done it yet. I'm not quite confident in swing trading overnight. They can fluctuate so much. I'm still kind of scared to do that.

Mostly I try to wait the first 30 minutes to an hour after the market opens. I wait for at least the first 30 minutes, because I've gotten into trouble there, and I take this time to see what's going on. I used to trade immediately when the market opened. It can go either way obviously, so I try to wait, but I don't have a specific set time.

It can be the middle of the day and I'll jump into a trade.

Jane: Do you know of any other female traders besides me that you follow online or anywhere else? Are there any other women that you see in the day trading world?

Ashley: No.

Jane: I was trying to do research and basically they say it's 10% of day traders that are successful, and if I look at the people who follow me, it's 12% women. That means that by being a successful day trader and a woman, you're in 1.2% of day traders, which is ... It's crazy. It should be at least 50%. 50/50.

Ashley: Yes, I agree.

Jane: Well, is there anything else you want to add that you'd like other women to know in going forward, or any questions that you have for me?

Ashley: No, I think I got it.

Jane: It's all good stuff because it's great perspective for someone to see a newer trader. I want to do all ranges. I have some women that have their own educational trading programs. It's great to see the whole gamut of the range of women day traders, because when I was getting into it, I only saw Tim Sykes online. I didn't see any females out there. I think it's really important to try to help others.

Ashley: Yeah, I definitely agree. It's definitely an untapped market as far as I've seen.

Jane: Wonderful. Ashley, I'm here. If you ever have any questions, feel free to send me messages. I really appreciate your time. I hope I didn't pull you away from your son while he's screaming or needing your attention. Honestly I'm here to help you too if I can. I still feel like you, and I started back in February 2015. Today I made over $2000, but I still feel like I have a lot to learn as well because it's just the nature of the game.

Ashley: Right.

Jane: I feel the more you know, the more you see you don't know.

Ashley: Yes, I would agree with that. I would definitely agree. I felt the more that I learn, it's just opening up more questions.

Jane: Okay, perfect. Do you mind if I ask your age of getting into it, so that my readers will see a range of ages?

Ashley: 31.

Jane: Awesome. I'm 39 myself.

Ashley:	Don't look it.
Jane:	Thank you. It's a lifetime of exercise and eating well.
Ashley:	Oh, good.
Jane:	Wonderful. Great. Thank you so much, Ashley. I really, really appreciate it, and I will keep you up to date as the project comes along.
Ashley:	All right, great. Well it's great talking to you.
Jane:	Good talking to you; have a wonderful night.

Jordan Taylor

Global Traveler – Home base USA

Instagram: Travellight21
Twitter: @Travellight_
YouTube: https://www.youtube.com/Travellight21

I first discovered Jordan through her Instagram account. I saw one of her posts about trading and traveling. There are many men who post trading from hotels or beaches around the world, but Jordan was the first woman I saw in the public eye. Intrigued, I reached out to learn more about her story.

Jane: Describe your journey to trading. Was it always part of your life? Did you learn from your family?

Jordan: No. I really just found out about it probably two-and-a-half years ago. I just started researching the stock market completely on my own out of curiosity. It wasn't really with the intent of starting to trade in the stock market. I was just interested in it. I had a friend who I knew was trading in the stock market. He was an independent trader. I said to him, "Hey, I started researching the stock market and I know you do it

21

and I'd really love to know more about it." So he just started showing me his process and I became more and more interested. I remember one day I realized, "Wait. People could do this without having millions of dollars, couldn't they?" And he said, "Well, yeah." And so at that point, I thought, "All right. This is something I want to do." So I shifted my research toward it being something that I would pursue myself.

Jane: Now when you started researching, were you in college, or had you already graduated? Your voice sounds pretty young, so I'm just curious. Where were you in your life when you found out about trading? Because I am interviewing a different age range of people. I'm due to be 40 next August.

Jordan: Oh, from your picture, I thought you were in your 20s.

Jane: Oh, thank you!

Jordan: No. I'm 27, so this would've been when I was 24, 25-ish. I went to university to get an English degree. I didn't end up finishing but it was really nothing to do with the stock market at all. So my degree wasn't related to trading.

Jane: Now when you got started, did your friend really help mentor you?

Jordan: Yeah. I would consider him a mentor. He kind of had a very different approach to the stock market that I adopted. He would tell me, "There are so many technicalities and everything, but I'm just going to teach you the basics," and he did. And I didn't really learn about more of the technical stuff until later, when I was already trading. I don't know if that was good or bad, but it ended up working out for me.

Jane: Now was his style more of swing-trading, value-trading? How would you describe the style?

Jordan: Swing-trading. But he would basically just buy low and sell high. I know that's very basic but that is what he would do and he would kind of oversimplify things. I think that really helped me when I was starting out. So, that was beneficial.

Jane: And when you started, did you have any tools that you used, like any DVDs or books, or anything like that?

Jordan: I read some books on the stock market. But I can't even remember their titles. None of them really stood out for me. I know I learned things from them, but I would just go to my friend and say, "Hey, what's this?" And he would always have a very extremely simplified way of understanding everything and explaining it. I guess I just got more from his explanations. I know it's bad but I really can't even remember the names of the books.

Jane: That's totally fine. It's like going to school for your degree and then you go out into the real world and you do an internship. In my opinion it's the hands-on experience with the market that really helps educate you instead of what you can just read in a book. Even though books are great for value, it's not the only source that you're going to have.

Jordan: Yeah, and I would always get more out of articles actually. I have all these things on Facebook that I tag that I want to read about: stock market, finance, investing.

All these articles will pop up and I actually find that I get more out of those.

Jane: And now you basically just travel the world trading for enjoyment, right?

Jordan: Yes.

Jane: What is your setup that you travel with? What do you look for in setting up a trading site while you're on the road traveling?

Jordan: In terms of how do I trade and still travel?

Jane: Yes, but obviously you have certain hardware that you take with you. Do you have a laptop and monitors? When you're trying to figure out where you want to stay? Do you research and say, "Okay, I have to make sure that I have internet at least X amount of time"?

Jordan: Exactly! Yes! That's really important. So as for what I have, I only have a laptop. It's a MacBook Air. I haven't had any problems; it's awesome. When I research where to go, yes, internet is essential. Before I've made the mistake of saying, "Oh, they have internet? That's good enough for me." And then they might only have it downstairs in the lobby of a hotel where it might not be fast enough to load my Think or Swim platform which is always bad. Now I have them actually screenshot their speed test before I will commit to staying there.

Jane: Very thorough. Do you typically just trade in your hotel, or will you go out and trade? You see some people who post, "I'm trading by the pool," or "I'm trading out on the beach." Now it's your way of life, so I'm sure you've sharpened it up to perfection as to how your day is structured.

Jordan: Yes, I do trade on my phone. I really like TD Ameritrade for that and it depends on the day. If I think something is going to happen, then I might not go out. I watch the market. The time difference of where I am in the world also makes a difference. Sometimes I'll put in limit orders if I know that I'm going out exploring. I stay at mostly Airbnbs now because they have better privacy and better Wi-Fi than hotels in general.

Jane: Okay and because you obviously have different time zones that you deal with, how do you set up your trading day? Sometimes it's the middle of the day, sometimes it's the evening, but do you have a particular routine that you follow before you go into your trades? Are there specific times you trade the US market?

Jordan: Sometimes I will buy or sell on pre-market, but not regularly. I only trade the US Market, but I am invested in some foreign stocks. I like emerging markets. I have an ETF with those stocks. Then with the time difference, I really just adjust my day around it and hopefully it's not too big of a difference. If it is, then limit orders come in handy.

Jane: Do you have a particular routine? Like for me, my day is always get up, feed my daughter, take her to daycare. I sit down at my computer like 9:12-ish. The time of the US market open hours in your location will be different based on the time zone of your destination. Say if you are in Thailand and trading, it would be 9:30 am in the US and 8:30 pm in Thailand. Do you have a particular routine that gets your mind set to trading?

Jordan: I always have my laptop set to New York time. Probably around 8:00 am New York time I'll start reading the news. I like to just keep up-to-date on world news and things that are going on in general. Then I look at the news for the stocks that I am holding. The CNBC app is really good for that. I can just go to all of the stocks that I have marked and that I have in my portfolio. Then the app gives me all the news on those stocks that are related to them. I kind of browse through my positions and have a coffee. It's really through this process that I enjoy starting the day. And I don't do that every day. It varies, but that's my approach in the morning.

Jane: It gets you in the trading zone.

Jordan: Yeah, sometimes I'm not trading in the morning.

Jane: Now you said you use Think or Swim and TD Ameritrade. Do you just trade with two accounts, or you have some other ones that you use for different items? I have three accounts because I have a 401k that I made to be self-directed and then I have two other trading accounts.

Jordan: I just have the TD Ameritrade. I do have a Vanguard account, but that one pretty much does itself and I don't pay any attention to it.

Jane: Got it. And you were saying you use the CNBC News. Do you use any particular software, or scanning tools, or applications to help you alert or filter out stocks to trade?

Jordan: Not really beyond the CNBC app. No, I kind of like to keep it simple.

Jane: No, that's fine. And when you get into a trade... You say you're more of a swing-trader; I imagine that's great traveling the world. When you get into a trade, what are you looking at to get into that swing-trade?

Jordan: How long I hold a stock really depends. I'm just waiting to make a certain percentage normally that I have in mind. It may not be an exact number, but I just kind of have an idea of what I want to get out of it. I'd say normally I hold stocks from three days to a week. Sometimes a lot longer though. Sometimes I hold stocks for a month, two months, three months. That's not the norm, though.

Jane: Do you use any sort of indicators, or how do you determine what stock you want to go into for a swing-trade?

Jordan: Generally I would watch the stock for a little bit. I would study its charts, its 52-week highs and lows. And then I would wait in general for that stock to go down a big percentage. I like to buy when stocks are down, especially if it's for a reason that I think the stock can really come back from. That's backfired on me before. Like I bought Twitter when it went down from that $40 to... I forget what it even went down to, but I bought that. That was not good. In other cases it's worked out great. I bought Morgan Stanley even though there was kind of a little panic about that. I look for things that people are having an unnecessary panic about. There's been a slight bad earnings report or something that I don't think will affect everything in the company so...

Jane: I hear you. Now, when you're looking at CNBC, do you pick the stocks that have maybe been the biggest losers, and then you watch those?

Jordan: Yes. Possibly. I have a watch-list of a lot of stocks that I'm interested in and that I own. And then, there is a tab on the Think or Swim application that suggests stocks that it thinks you might be interested in, so I look at those as well.

Jane: Typically how many trades do you find yourself in at one time?

Jordan: At one time, like how many different stocks I'm holding?

Jane: Correct. How many stocks would you be swing-trading at once?

Jordan: Probably five to ten.

Jane: When you're going into your positions, do you go all in at once? Or do you put in 50% of your position and add?

Jordan: I really try to avoid going all in, ever. I like to buy, like you said, 50% or even less of a percentage. And then, I just feel really comfortable because if the stock goes down more I feel like I still have the ability to buy it if I choose to make that decision. But then if it goes up, it's also a win because I'm making money and I can sell it.

Jane: Got it. You'll say you'll enter and then if it tends to go down, you might add to it, so you'd be adding to a loser at that time. What do you use for your risk tolerance from your entrance? Is it a percentage or a dollar amount?

Jordan: I don't really have a specific number, and because of recent events, I am looking at changing that. My biggest mistake so far in trading has definitely been adding to losers too much. I don't have a specific number at the moment, but if I feel that the stock is just going down and taking too much of my capital, I guess that's what I really look for at this time. If so much of my capital is in this stock and being dragged down by it, and then I see other stocks that I watched and could have bought, I think, "Oh, look at that, if I had done it, I would have been making money, but instead I'm losing money on this one." Now I look at what my capital could be doing.

Jane: Do you add to your winners as they're going up, or do you just go ahead and let that position run?

Jordan: I'm more likely to just let it run. I will sometimes add to it, but normally I just wait and sell it. I like to see big percentage moves.

Jane: And what would be considered a big percentage move to you?

Jordan: Well, one of my most volatile stocks used to move 20% in a day: NUGT gold triple-leveraged ETF. Yeah, that one's been pretty intense for me. That one is the stock that I've lost and made the most on.

Jane: What do you consider a big percentage gain to sell? Is it 10%, 15%? Obviously, that one, if it's doing 20% a day...

Jordan: That's not the norm. It'll take longer to get there, but I'd say even 10% is great.

Jane: Obviously you're holding your positions overnight. Do you tend to use hard stops or mental stops? If you're away from the computer, I would think it might be a hard stop, but do you use hard stops when you're trading? Or do you just assess it? Once you're in a trade, do you assess that trade throughout the day and monitor it on your phone? Or do you just look at it once a day and you reassess your portfolio daily?

Jordan: It's really a mixture of both, depending on the stock and depending on the day. I'm definitely checking my phone a lot while I'm out for the stocks moving one way or another. I prefer to do everything on my own to see a stock moving in a way that I'd like to buy or sell. Then I see that myself and I sell it. That's not always the case, but it's what I prefer.

Jane: You really aren't using limit orders too much except for like you said if you go out exploring and you know that you might not have the ability to put in an order.

Jordan: Yes. For example, I was in Costa Rica and there's really no internet beyond where you stay so I did do a few limit orders while I was there just because I knew there was no way I could even check the stocks during the day. I do feel most comfortable doing it myself and seeing what's happening as the stock moves throughout the trading day.

Jane: Now, it's really interesting that you say you use your phone a lot while you're abroad. Out of curiosity, do you have any sort of special plan or provider from the US that you find gives you the best option while you're abroad? Or do you actually buy SIM cards while you're abroad?

Jordan: I buy SIM cards. I have heard a few people say that... I can't even remember what carrier it is, maybe Verizon. I've heard somebody say that they found a really great plan that works for them abroad, but in my experience, that has never worked out for me. I'm kind of wary of that. If that existed it'd be great. But I haven't found anything like that yet that works. Especially because I'm switching countries so much, I just buy SIM cards.

Jane: It's amazing to be able to travel, and trade, and have the freedom to do so. Now how often do you end up setting up a base? Are you usually in a new city once every week? Or you go somewhere for a month? I'm just curious to see how it affects your trading.

Jordan: Normally, I would stay in a place for about a month. It really depends. I'm in Dubai right now for two weeks. After this, I plan to go to Bali, and I actually plan to settle there for three months, maybe even longer, specifically to get my trading account to the next level. It is difficult to do that when you're out all day and you can't sit at the computer and watch the market. I was in Mexico for three months; I lived in an apartment there. After that, there was a lot of traveling around, maybe a week here, two weeks there.

Jane: Very cool. That's awesome; it's amazing. I would love to do that, but with one daughter and another one on the way it's a little tough. Now, as far as your trading experience, do you remember your biggest loss?

Jordan: Yeah, it was definitely with NUGT. I guess this would be around two years ago. I was really new to trading. I was in NUGT a lot, and I was really excited by the stock. It was the first triple-leveraged ETF that I started investing in and it would just move up and down like crazy. It was very exciting so I was buying a lot of it. It was right around the $12 mark; that was probably where it was settled.. I was buying a lot there, and then I saw it go down to 10. I saw it go down to eight. I saw it go down to six. I saw it go down to five. And I didn't sell;

that was a mistake. It ended up coming back later after I had held it for a year. I guess it didn't end up being a loss in the end, because I kept it. But I shouldn't have kept it because I would've done a lot better investing the capital elsewhere. That was definitely a hard year.

Jane: And now, on the flip side, do you remember your biggest win?

Jordan: My biggest win was also with NUGT and this would have been not that long ago, it was probably in April of 2016. NUGT was moving like crazy. I was studying the charts, so it would kind of do a similar thing every day or every few days where it would go down a lot and then it would go up. So, I bought it, I think, at 91. And it actually went up to 125, and I made I think a 35% profit... I don't remember the percentage I made. But I made a lot more than I normally do on a trade. And that was in two days that it gained so drastically.

Jane: That's wonderful. Congratulations. Now when you're trading, do you use social media like Twitter or StockTwits to get information, or is it as you said looking at Facebook articles? Do you use Twitter or StockTwits at all with your trading?

Jordan: No, I really don't. I'm pretty new to Twitter. I use Instagram and YouTube a lot more.

Jane: Okay.

Jordan: I pretty much only opened an account because I actually bought some of their stock, but I don't use Twitter that often.

Jane: Got it. And do you use level two with yourThink or Swim platform? Or are you more looking at and reading the charts?

Jordan: Just the charts, mainly.

Jane: As a female coming into the trading world, have you found that there were any hurdles for you, like with family and friends supporting you? Or any other struggles in being a female?

Jordan: Yes. How I trade. I don't work at a company or anything like that, so, it's really often just me in my pajamas at home. So, it's not that I have a work environment really, but I do notice that when I tell people [what I do], they don't take me seriously. I've met a few people who are knowledgeable about trading and I would want to talk to them, but I would notice that... first of all, they'd all be men and I would really notice that they wouldn't take me seriously and they wouldn't even want to really discuss it with me. After I posted the videos on YouTube about my trading, I got a lot of super negative comments about how women can't trade, how all of this is a cover for something: "She's not really a trader", "She can't be a trader, she's too young, she's too pretty, she's a girl", whatever that is. And then I look at similar videos on YouTube in which men are saying the exact same things as me and there's absolutely none of that.

Jane: I get that too on my Twitter account. And the way I look at it is that they hate on us because we are successful in something that they want to be successful in. I believe they think less of themselves, so they have to turn out and lash out. I look at it this way: "You must really hate your life just because you're taking time out of your day to bash mine. Thank you."

Jordan: Yes.

Jane: I try to look at the flip side and the positive of it.

Jordan: Definitely, you have to.

Jane: Anything else you would say to a woman coming into the trading world?

Jordan: You can't let any negativity get you down. And there's really no reason that a woman can't trade. I don't think it's even a factor. It shouldn't be.

Jane: That's exactly how I think. It's a person behind the computer and the market, so it doesn't matter whether you are a male or a female. What matters is your knowledge on the subject.

Jordan: Exactly.

Jane: You don't have any children, and your home life is diverse as you're traveling around on the road.

Jordan: Yes.

Jane: How long would you say it took you to feel successful in your trading experience from when you started two-and-a-half years ago?

Jordan: It was probably earlier this year that I really started making enough money on the market to support myself.

Jane: Okay.

Jordan: Originally when I left to travel, I planned to leave for three months. And after three months I was going to go back home. But I was depressed to even think about that. I did not want to go back home; I wanted to keep traveling. I realized one day that I was doing really well on the market, and that I was good at it. I just realized I can do this as a career and I'm not going to be saving that much as I was living in Miami. I'd have to take money out of my account, which I didn't like doing before. But it kind of hit me like, "I'm making enough that I can support myself doing this." And I think that's when I really thought of myself as a trader, "Okay. I'm doing a good job. I'm good at this, I can do it." So, that's pretty cool.

Jane: Amazing! Before your success earlier this year, were you working a nine-to-five job or a part-time job while you were also trading?

Jordan: Yes. I was a manager at Starbucks. I was working 45-50 hours a week at a regular job.

Jane: And your style and strategy are still the same; it's just now you have more time to do it?

Jordan: I had scheduled my job to take the night-shift so I would go into work at around 5:00 pm and I'd work until 1:00 or 2:00 in the morning. It was perfect. The market would close and then I'd get ready for work. No one else wanted that shift, but I was like, "No, it's perfect for me."

Jane: Great thinking. Do you think that you became more consistent? Or did you see that the profits were enough where you could actually sustain it as a career?

Jordan: More of the second one. I just saw that I was making enough in profits. The more capital you have to invest, the larger your profit potential. So, I just built up my account. I didn't take money out of it until this year. So, I built up my account and got it to the level that I could survive off of it, on a modest level.

Jane: Very nice. And, if you don't mind me asking, how much did you start with when you first started trading two-and-a-half years ago?

Jordan: I had saved up $10,000. After I researched the market, and was mentored by my friend, he advised me not to put in all the money at once, which was very wise advice. So, I put in I think $2,000 or $3,000 and I was doing well. I wanted to make sure that I wasn't going to be trading too emotionally and that I wasn't going to be getting greedy. Those were really the two things that the mentor, friend of mine warned me about by saying, "People react to money, so you have to make sure that this is something you'll be ready for..." I thought I handled it well and I really enjoyed it. So, I put in the rest of the money. Over a month, I did that, so $10,000 was my initial investment.

Jane: And how much had it grown to once you made trading become your full-time career?

Jordan: Earlier this year, when I was making enough that I figured out I could live off it, it was around $45,000.

Jane: And during the first year-and-a-half, or today, do you analyze your trades at all in any way? Do you keep a trading journal where you track performance?

Jordan: Mm-hmm, I do. I really love lists and statistics and all that stuff. I'm very analytical; I enjoy it. So, I have a notebook full of all my trades. It has percentages, notes, dates. All that stuff is on my TD Ameritrade but I like to see it laid out in my notebook. In my own writing.

Jane: So you use an actual hard copy notebook? You don't use any sort of software that will analyze the trades for you besides your TD Ameritrade?

Jordan: My TD Ameritrade does all of the analyzing as well, but I like to write things down myself. Writing is part of my process.

Jane: Now that you've found success in trading, do you think this has affected your personal relationships at all? Have you felt like being successful in the market has affected your relationships? Besides the haters...

Jordan: Not really. The haters on YouTube are a whole different story, but no, I don't think so. I love talking about the market; I love telling younger people about it. I would always be talking about it at work when I worked at Starbucks. Where was I going with this? Okay, my current boyfriend, who I met while I was traveling, I actually started teaching him a little bit about the market and now he wants to start... And he's happy for me. Whenever I have a big winning trade, we celebrate. He does his own work online and that was kind of inspired by him seeing that I could do it. So, he found something that he could do online and now he travels with me. I think it's been a good thing.

Jane: That's great. Now, how has your family received it? Is your family excited for you as well, that you have this opportunity that you've created for yourself, where you can travel the world?

Jordan: Yeah. In general, they are. My dad is always really doubtful about it. I think he has a different idea of trading, that it's not something you do just on your computer; it's something that a professional does. I would tell him the average percent that I would make a year on my investments and he'd say, "Oh that's impossible." I'm like, "Okay." But my mom is always just really proud of me and bragging about me.

Jane: That's great.

Jordan: So she's happy for me. My dad is too, but he has his own perspective about trading.

Jane: Of course, well, did they grow up doing investing themselves? I imagine it was probably more value investing that they grew up with as some sort of influence if they had any at all.

Jordan: Well, my dad used to work at a Fortune 500 company, and he used to have the option to trade their stocks. And he would do it, but it was a very long process. And I think he ended up losing a lot of money. So this would have been 20, 30 years ago. And I think that colored his perception a bit.

Jane: Is there anything that you would say to a new trader coming to the market that you would absolutely recommend that they follow in starting out?

Jordan: Well first of all, I would say that if they're just trying to make some quick cash, to abandon the project. Just don't do it, because that's not what the stock market is for. I would tell them to really do their own research to decide what strategy they want to use because there's so many different strategies. There's no one right way to trade the stock market. I feel like there are a lot of articles that are going to try and tell you, "You have to do this. You cannot do this." And there's a lot of great advice out there. But they just have to really do their own research, form their own opinions, and come up with their own strategy. I think that's really important. And not be too emotional about the stocks either.

Jane: Do you have any particular rules that you always follow when you're trading? I actually have mine framed on my desk just to remind me. They're right in front of my face.

Jordan: Well, they're not really written down rules, but I do have some... I think number one would be not to take stock tips. And I found that when your friends hear that you're on the stock market, they all have this stock that you just have to go and get. And that has never ever, ever worked out, so I never take stock tips from people. I try not to get caught up in a stock. I do take some risks, but I just don't like to get caught up all in the emotion of a stock. "And oh my gosh, look at how it's moving. Look at all the money I could be making." I feel like that's what I did in the beginning with my biggest loss with NUGT, and it did not end well, so...

Or, the thing that happened with Twitter, I don't know if you remember. It must have been a year-and-a-half ago when they hacked the numbers, and they came out early. And ever since, Twitter has never been the same. There was this huge frenzy on the market that actually shut down the market early. And I got caught up in that. I thought, "Oh my gosh, look how much Twitter is going down. I'm going to buy some." I saw it going down more. And I just got so excited. I actually bought more shares of it. Those shares never recovered, and ended up to be pretty big losses. So I try to stand back a little, not get caught up, and really analyze it.

Jane: Would you say that before with your swing trades, you were trading based on the pullbacks? Are you looking for stocks that are say, pulling back from the 52-week high, and then you enter in as it pulls back or it's in the mid-range, and then it pulls back down 30%, and then you look to enter? How do you assess your entry? Is it a high stock that's at the 52-week high, pulled back, and you enter there, or is it one that's oversold that's hitting new 52-week lows? What is the main indicator to go in for you?

Jordan: I like for a stock to be in the mid-range of its 52-week high. I feel like there is room to move around. And from there, I will watch it. I watch for it to drop. I might watch for it to drop and then see how it comes back, because I like stocks with a lot of volatility. And then when it drops again, I would be more likely to buy it.

Jane: Do you have any goals for your trading as far as you want to just keep it yourself and travel the world, or do you want to end up educating or running a site on it? I know you're big into YouTube and advertising your trading abilities there. Is there any goal that you look forward to achieving with your trading?

Jordan: What I'm doing now was really the dream for me a year ago or two years ago. So I feel like I'm there right now, which is awesome. I don't really want to go down the path of advising people, particularly because I don't know all the technicalities with the market. I don't know how to put it, but I trade simply, so I don't feel like I would be the best person to actually teach people about the market. I just want to grow my account and keep being able to travel, really.

Jane: That's a great goal in itself to be able to have the freedom and financial freedom to travel the world and do your job that you love at the same time.

Jordan: Yup. It's a passion of mine. I really enjoy it.

Jane: That's what it's all about. I think that's what many people need to figure out. When you do it as a career, it needs to become a passion and not just a means to an end. There's a lot of energy that needs to go into it. And it won't just happen overnight - it takes time.

Jordan: Definitely.

Jane: Perfect, Jordan. Thank you so much, and have a great night. Thank you for participating. It's really exciting.

Jordan: Yes, thank you.

Jane Gallina

Canada

Twitter: @jane_yul
Instagram: missairplanejane
Facebook: @SugarAirplaneJane
Blog: www.seejanetrade.com
Website: www.carpeprofit.com
YouTube: Airplane Jane

This is an interview conducted by Jacob Whitish for his Digital Stock Summit in 2016. I had seen a post on Twitter about the summit and asked him more about it. I offered to be a female voice to add to his interviews if he wanted me to share my story. This interview helped fuel my drive to interview others and compile their stories together here in this book. The original video interview is available on Jacob's Youtube channel: Virtual Summit Media, LLC.

Jacob: All right, hey Jane, how's it going?

Jane: Great, how are you?

Jacob: Not too bad. I was actually ignoring stocks this morning, and then you told me you were watching

MGT here, and I had to go and take a look at that. Definitely pretty exciting and interesting.

Jane: Definitely.

Jacob: I had to actually close all my windows after you said that you did. I said to myself, "All right, I guess I'll put away mine too."

Jane: Well, I know for myself, if it's up, I'm going to watch it. So, I wanted to give you my full attention.

Jacob: We first met when I was running the initial week-long Digital Stock Summit. You found me, I don't even know how you initially found me, but you did. And you were probably one of the number one people driving traffic my way. And after we talked a little bit more, I said, "Holy crap! This girl is really cool. We've got to talk to her." Not too long after, you actually had mentioned being exactly that, being interested in doing an interview, and especially wanting to show other women that it is possible; it's not just a guy's game.

Jane: Definitely.

Jacob: So here we are. To get started, why don't you give us a little bit of background about yourself, explain what made you first become interested in stocks, and maybe provide a quick summary of how you've gotten to this point and where you're at now.

Jane: I've never been a nine-to-five person. Right after college, I started working in banking, but I didn't really like it. I found it a little boring. So, I thought, "Okay, I'm going to pick up and I'm going to try the stock market. It seems more interesting." So, I went and I got my series

7 and worked as a registered assistant. I was working at Smith Barney in Atlanta in the WorldCom Office where they had all their options. And unfortunately, they had advised the employees to go ahead and use margin against their options and then the stock tanked. So, a lot of the employees were underwater. I saw the devastation and I thought, "You know what? I am not sure that I want to work with other people's money." I went ahead and took a voluntary lay-off and I studied culinary school in Europe for a year instead. It was a wonderful change. Then I moved to Philadelphia and I started working in the culinary world, and I ran my own business as a wholesale pastry chef. When you have your own business, you also have to pay for insurance.

I also worked as well in customer service at the airlines, which is not a great-paying job; however, it covered my health insurance. When I was there, I met my husband, and he's from Canada. So, I moved up to Montreal and I kept my job with the airlines so that I would have a job once I immigrated to Canada. Once I was up here, we got married, had our first child, and I had a year of maternity leave. And I thought, "I really want to be present." Having a child changed my life. She became number one, and I wanted to figure out how I could be present for her and still provide income. And my husband was the one who actually reminded me that I'd had a great stock investment. I bought $25,000 worth of American Airlines when it was in bankruptcy. And then over the next nine months, they merged with US Airways, they re-issued their stock, and I ended up turning $25,000 into $250,000.

Jacob: Wow, way to go.

Jane: Thank you. I thought, "Yeah, I do love it. I love the numbers, I love doing the research, so maybe I should look more into this." And in this process I went ahead and started doing research online. When I came across Timothy Sykes' page, I thought, "This almost looks too good to be true. This might be bogus. I'm not sure about this." So, I started doing my research, and seeing reviews, and actually signed up as his challenge student. And I told my husband, "You know what? This is the time. I've got six months where our daughter is home. I can really study this and learn the ins and outs of it." I signed up, got accepted, and started studying. My daughter was about six months old at the time and I used to schedule her naptime around morning open so that I could be sitting at the computer to watch the open.

Well, it didn't work so well for me. I didn't follow rules. I went ahead and I started trading as soon as I opened up my account. I blew up a $6,000 account pretty fast. It was not working for me trying to follow Tim's patterns, but I did learn a lot of the basics from Tim. I put it on hold for about five months until September. Once my daughter went to daycare, then I had free time to really devote to watching the market, watching the patterns, and moving forward with stocks. I started doing that. I started to write stocks down and track their movement. I started to look at gappers for the days, and I would track them. I would put them in an Excel spreadsheet and I would see, "Okay, this one gapped up and this one gapped down." I would ask, "What is the trend for these? What typically happens?" For stocks that go up and they have a great gap up, okay, so it's maybe three days that it's going up and then you have people that are going to go ahead and take their gains. Sometimes, they'll go ahead, and if it's an overnight explosion of news, they might go ahead and start selling it at open if it went up after market.

For the gap downs, I would watch and I would wait because I figured, "Okay, they're the shorts." And they're going to cover, and that's going to create a bounce. So, I started watching for the reversals. And that's really my number one trade that I really enjoy because I see it setting up. I can almost feel the tension in the price movement on the level two and I also watch the three charts; one, two, and five minute charts for stock so that I can see when it switches from red to green on all three. That's usually an indicator for me: "Okay, go ahead and get in." Sometimes I'm not so good. Sometimes I get in early and I end up averaging down, but that's pretty much a little synopsis of me getting into the market and a little bit of what I do.

Jacob: Okay. I don't want get too far ahead of myself, but at this point, you have done well enough to earn yourself the nickname 'Sugar Jane', right?

Jane: Yes. Actually, my husband came up with that after I had my first absolutely amazing week where I had made $27,000. It was almost surreal because when I was working at the airlines up here, granted it was part-time, I was working 32 hours a week. I was waking up between 2:00 and 2:30 in the morning for a 4:00 am start, working 4:00 am to 8:00 am. I was making roughly $800 a month, part-time, working 120 hours in a month. So for me, it was like, "Is this really happening? Is this my new reality?" And it is, because I make roughly a thousand a day. That's my goal that I try to achieve. Some days I make it, some days I lose, but I know that every trade is a fresh trade.

Jacob: That is fantastic and I think we'll come back around and finish up talking about all of that a little bit more, but first I wanted to give everybody an early taste of where all this is going and then maybe give everyone some incentive to stick around.

Jane: Yes!

Jacob: I also want to touch on something really quickly. You said that you did a lot of research into Tim Sykes. What was it about him that drew you in? There are so many different services, so many different mentors, so many different gurus, so to speak, out there. What was it that made you feel like he was the right one for you?

Jane: Well, looking at his site, I was very interested in the penny stocks basically, because that's exactly what I did with American Airlines. I bought it at $2.51 and sold it basically up at 40. It was the long shot, the home run, it was the rarity, but it did happen and it did work for me and so I thought, "Okay, yes, I see that penny stocks are viable as a source of generating income; you don't have to trade the large cap stocks." My parents were always into value investing, so I actually grew up with them reading *The Wall Street Journal* every morning. I started learning about stocks, but it was always, in my parents' mind, a long-term investment. I wanted to be more proactive and work day-to-day. I really wanted to watch the price action and have my hands wet in it. Seeing Tim's site and seeing his honesty through his site, the positives and the negatives, and showing how people can learn from his negatives, really taught me a lot. I could see his faults in trading, so I wouldn't necessarily do them myself.

Some things like his rule, "Don't trade before you understand what's going on," yes, I had to learn the hard way, but I see that as my market tuition, you know? In learning, in going to school, you have to pay tuition. Well, that was my market tuition. But I try to help people not to let that happen and I suggest paper trading from the beginning. Once I started paper trading, I really learned how to execute trades including when to get in, when to get out, understanding the price action, and studying the market as opposed to just emotionally jumping into a trade. "This is going to work for me, I hope it's going to go there," isn't the reality.

Jacob: Okay. So you do see a lot of value in paper trading for yourself?

Jane: I do, definitely. I highly recommend it to everybody that follows me.

Jacob: Sure, and that was one of the things that I touched on several times throughout the summit, because it's such a polarizing issue. Some people are like, "Yes, it's great. It's a great way to learn and to understand what's going on," and then other people are like, "No, there's no emotional attachment to it. It's not the same." It sounds like you're definitely on the pro-camp. Where do you see it in terms of not having the emotional attachment, does that hurt people?

Jane: Well, I think it probably does hurt people a little bit, but if they use an automated online system likeThink or Swim or tradingview.com, then they can practice on digital software. And if someone's never traded before, they can learn how to put the trades in before they get in with real money so they're not as likely to lose. They won't be fumbling around asking, "How do I put in a sell? It's going against me, how do I stop this?" because they've had the practice of doing it online. As far as paper trading without emotions, I think until people actually use their real money, that is a changeover for them. They are going to start feeling the emotions and the struggles: "Uh-oh, it's going down two cents. Should I get out? Is this going to go against me?" That's going to happen for sure and you can't replace that with paper trading, but at least with paper trading, you can start to see the patterns. If you do it electronically, you can learn how to enter the trades.

Jacob: That's interesting. You're the first person who's touched on just the basic mechanics of how to use this platform. I haven't heard anybody mention that side of it before and you're absolutely right: that's a pretty important part.

Jane: Well, it's any software. You have to learn a new software in order to be able to trade. There's so much information in trading, why not do it in baby steps? Take a little bit each day and then go forward with it, instead of, "Okay, here are the keys." It's like getting keys to a car, and you're 13 years old, go ahead and drive. Well, you don't know the rules of the road, you don't know... You haven't learned anything except for, "Okay, accelerate, stop, maybe use my blinkers." But you haven't learned all the nuances, and so, in giving someone an account fresh off the bat without studying anything, or without testing it, they're going to more than likely blow it up.

I think that's the reason why 90% fail, because they don't take the time to learn through baby steps.

Jacob: Sure, I actually really loved that. That's something that I never would've really thought of, but it is a foundational component of what you're doing. When you're getting ready for your trading day, what does that look like? What kind of research do you go through to prepare? What time does it start? Is it the night before, or the day of?

Jane: Well, for me, I start my research at about 4:00 pm the day before. I'll go ahead and do a scan. And because I like gappers, I will see what has closed up high, and what's closed low for the day. And I go ahead and I mark that down and I'll see what has a high short float to it. Then I put it aside until after 8:00 pm. I'll go ahead and I'll see what has changed in after market hours. Because with my daughter, I pick her up at 4:30 pm from daycare after I do my scan. This is her time. I prioritize her. She goes to daycare because she absolutely loves it. I pick her up because I miss her, and I'm done with my day. So why not go ahead and pick her up, and we play, we have fun. But then she goes to bed around 7:00 pm, so I have an hour to relax and then I do my scans again after 8:00 pm. If it's a night where I'm doing my blog, I'll do my blog as well. I try to input my trades on Profit. ly. I do them throughout the day so that I don't take time away from my daughter or my family.

In the morning, I take care of her and then I drop her off at daycare. I should be back at my desk about 9:10 am. Then I boot everything up, and I look to see what's volatile that morning. I try to track what has happened from the day before, but after hours and pre-market really dictate what I'm looking at. Because if something's in play with volume, it's going to be liquid to get in and out. If it doesn't have any liquidity to it, depending on my size, I might get stuck and really get underwater, because I can't get out of the trade. So I always want a stock that's got a lot of volume to it. And because I do like trade reversals, I like to look and see what has gapped, so that I know that there's going to be a lot of opposition and reversing that's going to happen throughout the day.

Jacob: Okay. Do you typically go long or short on those?

Jane: I typically go long lately because of my broker. I don't always get shorts, so I look more for the longs because I know that I'm going to be able to execute an entry. If it's a short, I can get frustrated. I don't want to go into a trade or track a stock that I'm not going to be able to get into. I don't want to get frustrated and change my mindset for the day instead of getting a good entry into a stock.

Jacob: Sure. I know for me, it's more about the mentality. It's really hard for me to get into the mentality of thinking about why a company should go down instead of up.

Jane: Well, for me, it's the same reasoning. I look for the Bollinger Bands. If it's overextended, it's overextended, whether it's up in price action or down in price action. It's going to come back one way or the other, but I find that longs are easier to execute.

Jacob: Gotcha. That makes sense. Talk a little bit about the strategy of actually working with those trades. Are there any particular indicators that you like looking for, and how do you scale in and out?

Jane: For me, I look at the stock. Basically, I'll look at it at open. I try to sit on my hands until about 9:45-9:50 because, as I've tracked my trades in Profit.ly and written them down, I see that if I make an entry before then, it's usually going to go against me. If I go long, I usually do not profit. I try to wait until there's a clear reversal on the day, around 9:50. And because there's the morning panic. If it's gapped down, you have some short covers that are just going to execute immediately. So it's going to spike up a little bit, but then people are probably going to continue in the same direction and it's going to go ahead and continue down until about 10:00. And then it's going to go ahead and rebound. I look for the price action, and I also look for Bollinger Bands. If it completely tanks outside of the Bollinger Band, then I know that it's going to have the rubber band snapback effect, and it's going to go right back up pretty much to the bottom of the Bollinger Band.

I also look at RSI. I check the RSI on the one-minute chart, and I see, "Okay, well, it's beginning to be oversold." There's not a lot of liquidity then of the actual stock in the market, because you're only going to have so many shares that can trade hands and it's basic supply and demand. Once you've eliminated all the shares because people have sold them, then people are going to start scrambling, and they're going to start buying like crazy, and then it's going to go right back up. So, I use RSI and Bollinger Bands. Those are my two primary ones.

Jacob: I guess I also should've asked this back when we were talking about the research, but do you use any tools?

Jane: I actually did it the old school way, where I wrote down my trades in a book. I still write down my trades in a book and then I transfer them electronically. The parameters of my broker are not that great, but I had my initial value account there, so I just continued holding it there.

With scanning for stocks, I really like using Finviz and Trade Ideas. I like to look at their fundamentals, the screeners, and I put in my parameters there. I also use Trade Ideas throughout the day. If the stocks that I have picked in the morning are not performing, then I'm going to go ahead and look and see what else I have on my alerts in my Cloud with Trade Ideas. And I'm usually in the Trade Ideas trading room, throughout the day, so that I hear audibles because to me without having a chat room in the background, it's very lonely. I need to have somebody talking in order to be comfortable. I don't know why; it's just a personal thing.

Jacob: No, I get you. I work a hundred percent remote in all of the various jobs that I do. I was working from my apartment and found the exact same thing. I was very lonely, especially coming from a larger corporation. It was actually a government service, so it was very large. And now I'm in a co-working spot because I just found I like people around, even though I'm not working directly with them.

Jane: Yes.

Jacob: That's an interesting take on that. Finding a chat room just for that sound, that community, that comfort.

Jane: Definitely. And I learn through auditory as well, so if I hear an audible alert from somebody, "Hey, check out this stock," like "CWEI, it's breaking out today," then I'll go and I'll look at it too. I'm not necessarily going to enter, but it gives me the audible alerts.

Jacob: Okay, interesting. Trade Ideas seems like they're a very new company, right?

Jane: They have actually been around since 2002. They're actually going on *Shark Tank* this Thursday.

Jacob: Oh, cool!

Jane: Sorry, they're going for the interview this Thursday.

Jacob: The interview, okay. Yeah, 'cause it seems like maybe the last few months out of nowhere, they've just appeared and everybody is suddenly talking about them. I don't want to plug any particular company or service too much, but it sounds like they're one of your main tools?

Jane: Definitely, I really enjoy using them. I'm still part of Tim's site, and I still watch his videos, his daily recap videos, and his watch list, but one of his main ideas is to teach traders the basics and then have them go on to basically fend for themselves. To create their own watch list and execute their own trades. That's what I've done. A lot of people say, "Well, you don't trade like Tim Sykes; why do you recommend him?" I say, "Well, because that's his idea." For me, trading is finding the niche that works for you. Whatever your comfort level is, whatever your risk tolerance is, you have to find the trades that make you comfortable. If you try doing what other people do, it's not necessarily being honest with yourself, and you're going to execute those trades poorly. It's just going to blow up and go against you because you're trying to do something that's not you, if that makes sense.

Jacob: Sure. So, really quickly, what is it about Trade Ideas that really made you such a big fan about them versus other tools?

Jane: Well, with Trade Ideas, they have so many different options and parameters... They have about 19 different alert pages and then you can also set up your own alerts. You can create your own alert that's going to scan all of the stocks. They're going to see whatever your price action is. However you set up your parameters, it's going to let you create a list so that you get a pop-up when that stock meets your criteria. And they also have a back tester so you can see the probability of your alerts providing profitable trades. "Okay, for me, I like to have the bottom bouncers that have potentially hit 52-week lows within the past three days and I love Fridays because people tend to close their shorts." So I watch those stocks throughout the week that have hit the 52-week low, and I see how active they are. And I'll set up parameters to find those bottom bouncers.

It's great because whatever your parameters are, you can customize them. If you don't want to customize them, they also have an artificial intelligence. They have stocks that are on the move in social media. They have stocks that are gapping up, stocks that are gapping down. They have ETFs. They have all sorts of things. There's something for everybody in it. It's not just one scanning software. It's customizable to you, and if you want to talk in the trading room, then they have a page too where other traders exchange ideas. They have a Cloud where you can exchange your link to your scanning alerts, so you can share it with everybody. Or you can also put in price alerts, and you can share those too. There are just so many options. I find it so amazing because it's not limited to just say charting and price alerts on the chart.

Jacob: So it's really that flexible and that customized?

Jane: Yes.

Jacob: Perfect. How many of these stocks are you typically looking at in any particular day or hour?

Jane: For myself, I will usually be in about three stocks maximum just because it's a lot to watch. I'd say the entry is the most crucial part for me because if it's a reversal, I want to try to enter at the bottom. Of course, everybody says that but it's difficult. And I always think of Warren Buffet's saying, "I know I'm going to mess it up but it's..." I don't remember what it is, but essentially you should buy when everybody else is panicking.

Jacob: Be greedy when others are fearful.

Jane: There you go. Be greedy when others are fearful. Because then, you're going to get the discount. To me, I told my husband this, "You know, I'm a bargain shopper." It's funny that's turned out to be my strategy in stocks. I like to find the oversold value stocks pretty much. Or stocks that have some value that are in action. I go and I buy those when they're undervalued. And wait for them to bounce up.

Jacob: Do you typically hold things overnight or do you just close out at the end of each day?

Jane: It depends. If it's a stock that has had a lot of sell-offs throughout the week and it's closing strong to the day, I will hold it overnight because I'm holding it in anticipation of shorts covering and gaping it up in the morning.

Jacob: Okay. I guess, along with those kinds of plays that incur a lot of a risk, what do you do to try and protect yourself from any potential negative eventuality?

Jane: Well, I try to use hard stops which I've really been doing actually since Friday. I was seeing that I was just letting things run against me. I was bad about not necessarily cutting my losers when I should, which of course is going to help to retain the profits. So I started to really use hard stops to protect my profits as it's running up but also to protect myself so that I'll take a minimal loss when it's going down if it goes down any further.

Jacob: How do you decide where you put those stops?

Jane: I look at the support lines and I also look at the obvious. If the stocks are up at $0.66, whatever, $13.66, well, I know that $13.50 is probably going to be a point of support if it's not already on the chart. So I'll put it in at 49, just below that so that I don't get stopped out too early. But I allow myself some leeway so that if it's a $1.50 to the upside and $0.16 to the downside, my risk reward is much greater. So my reward is much greater than my risk. I'm going to go ahead and let it go down that little bit.

Jacob: Okay. Fair enough. I guess also on that subject of losses, what was one of your biggest losses so far?

Jane: One of my biggest losses was actually BABY. I let it go $9,000 against me. Yeah, yeah. That was after my

$27,000 week. So I think I got a little overconfident and I had an emotional entry. I thought, "Oh, yeah, I had a great Friday. This is wonderful." And that was a Monday and I was just like, "You know what?" And I ended up holding it for a week and closed it out the next Monday because I thought, it's not coming back. I'm being a bag holder here. I can use this money to go forward with something else instead of just letting it sit there and lose.

I went ahead and cut it and it was a mental thing over the weekend. I accepted it. All the stages of grief. I had to look and say, "Okay, it's not getting better. I need to just accept this. I need to go ahead and cut the loss." Because there's more potential with the money than just letting it sit there and lose. As hard as it is to accept a loss, I went ahead and cut it and just moved forward because every trade is a new trade and I learned from my mistake. Now, I'm trying to be better with my stops and protect myself.

Jacob: What advice would you give to somebody else in a similar situation?

Jane: Well, I would say, try not to get yourself into that situation. But if you do break your rules, go ahead and cut the loss. It could come back, but it could also get exponentially worse. And if you've accepted it and you're okay with it, just go ahead and cut it because you can use that capital to make money instead of just sitting there and continuing to lose.

Jacob: Have you checked on BABY since?

Jane: No, I haven't really actually.

Jacob: I was going to ask you a follow-up on that. Have you looked back?

Jane: Now, I'm going to see. I'm going to check really quickly.

Jacob: And how long ago was that?

Jane: Oh yeah, well yeah, it would have come up. Let's see, April 19th. That happened middle of... Let's see, I think it happened, I'd say it happened about April 11th and then it looks like April 19th or 20th, I would have gotten out at a profit but...

Jacob: So if you held it two weeks instead of one it wouldn't have been so bad.

Jane: Exactly.

Jacob: But you don't recommend that obviously. In the meantime, that would've been a whole lot of red on your screen that would've been just making you feel awful.

Jane: Exactly. Every time I'd come to my computer, it wouldn't have been a positive. I think a lot... I was talking with Mandi, a fellow trader in Australia, and a lot if it is also mental mindsets. If you're thinking about negativity, then you're not going to be clear-headed to go forward and execute a trade very well. So if I have that... Even if I have a disagreement with my husband or something or conflict or I'm running late and I sit down at my desk late at say 9:16 or 9:18, it really actually affects my day because I'm not on par and I'm not clear-headed. I'm distracted in a certain way. In the same way, I also do yoga and yoga is very much about being present in the moment and I find that's the same with trading. You have to be present in the moment and the price action, not hoping or wanting the price to do something for you but to actually be in that price action. And if it's going against you, cut it. If it's going up and you're long, that's something else. I have to get better at letting the trades continue to rise because I see the profit and I'm like, "Oh great, yeah, it's going all right. Wonderful." And then I just... I feel the beginning of tension and I go ahead and I lock the profit.

Jacob: I guess on the flipside, was that $27,000 week your biggest week so far?

Jane: Yes, it was, and my biggest month too.

Jacob: So right now, we're sitting in May 2016, and you said you started back in November 2015 really truly focusing on it.

Jane: Yes, I started back in November to really focus on trading by doing my paper trading. Well, in September, I did paper trading. By November, I went to real money very small to try to gain my confidence with winning trades and gain my confidence in seeing that my trades were... I had better trades than losses. And then in January, I brought my account profits out of a negative and I started to have mostly profits really on my profit chart.

Jacob: Okay, and so it's really only been about six or seven months since you've really truly focused on it and that's huge in such a short amount of time.

Jane: Yes.

Jacob: I pulled MGT up while you were looking up BABY.

Jane: I got stopped out at 0.94.

Jacob: Yeah, it would've been up. It did in fact do exactly what you said, just not as big. So before we got started on this recording, you were watching MGT. You were waiting for that 3.10 and got stopped out just as we were preparing, so we went ahead. Maybe I should let you go a little further.

Jane: No, no, no, of course not. No, I had my stop and I was okay with that. Now, you made me curious, yeah.

Jacob: Well, it's 3.16ish right now.

Jane: Yeah, and at 3:00 pm, the shorts are going to start to have short calls. It's probably going to continue up the rest of the day. Actually, I might go and place a little trade while we're talking.

Jacob: Go for it. Go for it. Are you a fan of using social media in your trading research?

Jane: Definitely. Well, for myself, I wasn't on Twitter at all until I joined Timothy's trading challenge. One of the things that he recommended was definitely to open a Twitter account, so I went ahead and opened a Twitter account. I thought well, I'm going to follow some people. I followed Tim. I followed a couple of other people. I thought well, I don't really use this. And then later, I started posting what I was doing as a price alert system. As I started to gain in my profits, I started to gain in my followers too. I actually just broke 3,000 followers today.

Jacob: Nice.

Jane: Thank you. It's great because I really enjoy helping people and from the demographics of my Twitter followers, I see it's 87% men and 13% women. I feel like it should be more 50-50. Obviously, I do think it's a male-dominated field because many women don't think to do it. They don't think, "Oh well, let me sit down and learn stocks." I think the stigma is it's just a male field, but in reality, men and women are the exact same behind a computer screen. It doesn't matter. There's no glass ceiling or anything. It's just yourself and the computer, and the stock market, and the price action. There's no reason why a woman should be fearful to study, learn, try, and see if trading is a good fit for them.

Jacob: Why do you think that is? Why do you think there's such a discrepancy in the gender balance?

Jane: I think it's more just that women don't think to try it. It's not something that they would necessarily say, "Okay, well, I'm going to sit down and I'm going to go ahead and I'm going to try day trading." They might look at more value investing which I think female value investors are fairly well-represented. I don't know the breakdown percentages of male to female investors in value trading. You have Suze Orman who's a big promoter of female investors. As far as day trading, especially with all the movies too, it is typically portrayed as all men. There really aren't that many books out there either about female day traders and I think it's important to try and inspire women. I've been at it six, seven months, like you said. Even if I have a big failure, I'm going to try to learn from it. I'm going to share that, so that others can learn as well, because it's not something that women should be fearful of trying. You can learn anything. If you can learn a new language, you can learn chart patterns.

I spoke with a nurse about how she's been trading, and she says, "You know, looking at a chart is like looking at a heartbeat for me. I just start to see the patterns and it makes sense." But a lot of people don't realize that they can bring experiences from their life into trading. I'm also an Instrument-Rated Pilot, so doing a scan of different charts and price action is natural to me. And I think it'd be very easy actually for other pilots because of that reason. It's just something that they're used to in their day-to-day life.

Jacob: What do you see as some of the biggest hurdles that are really preventing women from getting on board? Is there anything specific to women do you think? Or is it just that it's so portrayed as a male industry?

Jane: I think it's just that women don't think to get into it. I just went into MGT. They don't necessarily say, "Oh hey, guess what, I'm going to learn how to day trade today." Or they might not actually look for research. Oh! MGT is up to 3.25. I think it's just something that they don't think about every day, as in, "I'm going to go into this field," when they could very easily do so.

Jacob: Okay. What advice would you give, especially as a new female trader, for any new trader who is looking to get into trading, or maybe just has a little interest and doesn't really know much about it?

Jane: I set up a page on my blog about this. A good time-line for new traders is basically to go ahead and find a mentor, whoever that might be. Find someone that you can follow and trust who will help you. Begin paper trading. Study the market, whether that is via books, or DVDs, or webinars, however you want to do it. Or even go to chat rooms. Just listen in a chat room. Go ahead and study the market and paper trade before you get in with real money so that you understand the market; you understand what's going on. As exciting as it is to want to jump in and do those trades, it's really a detriment to do it without any knowledge. Although you can get lucky just executing trades here and there, you're probably going to end up losing right off the bat if you don't study and learn the information.

Jacob: As a follow-on to that, of course, you can have all the information in the world, but then at the end of the day, you still have to pull the trigger and deal with your own emotions surrounding trading. How do you deal with those emotions?

Jane: Well, for me, I'd say I try to go ahead and protect my trades now with stops. If it went against me, okay, I'm going to go ahead and accept that stop. It's really difficult. That $9,000 loss was really tough to handle, but I definitely learned from it. And I know that I'm not perfect. I am human. I'm not a computer. I'm going to have days where my trades are not going to be the best, but I'm not going to try to force trades then. I'm just going to go ahead and wait for the trade setups to come to me. And emotionally, if I'm not with it, I really try not to revenge trade and go into a stock and say, "Oh, well, this stock owes me, because I lost on it." No, I'm going to stop, step back, watch, and see if there's a setup. I'm not going to force anything. If my mind is hung up emotionally on a trade, I'm not going to be able to execute it well, and I'm not likely going be able to profit from it.

Jacob: And that would definitely be really good advice for life.

Jane: Yeah.

Jacob: Stop, take a breath, see what's going on. But yeah, and especially in this with the markets, it's said pretty often that "The markets will just amplify whatever is already in you." If you're an angry person, you're going to be very angry. If you're a happy person, you'll probably be pretty happy. Only you'll experience those highs and lows so much more, and they're only going to show you the weaknesses that you already have. If you're particularly anxious, or you're really eager, then you're not good at having patience, and it's going to show you that. The market is going to show you that through a lot of bad trades.

Jane: Definitely. I do think it's a reflection of who you are in the market, and how you deal with your trades. If you have a loss, the best thing I can say is, "Learn from it." Don't beat yourself up, because, especially in the beginning, you're not an expert. You have so much to learn that you're expected to end up making errors. Learn from them. Don't beat yourself up about them.

Jacob: As we start wrapping things up, do you have any rules that you use, either mental or written down, that you refer to when you're doing your trades?

Jane: I have times that I don't want to enter the market. I don't want to go long at about 10:30 in the day. From my past trades, I see that when I go long, it usually goes against me. Same thing in entering the market long before 9:50; I just try not to do it because it will go against me. Let's see, what else? I try to cut my losers fairly quickly. And what else? I have my rules written down over here; let's see. Take time to watch to get into an entry. Don't be emotional about it. Is it a pattern that I recognize? What's the risk-reward ratio there? Is it something that is going to be a benefit to me getting in right there, or is it going to tank against me? And what is the benefit to the trade?

Jacob: Perfect. I think that's a great way to wrap things up. If anybody is interested in learning more about you, getting in touch, or reading your blog, what's a good way to find you and where?

Jane: Well, I'm on Twitter as @jane_yul or AirplaneJane. You can see my picture there. I have my blog, seejanetrade. com, and I am also on Instagram. I have a Facebook page as well and I am on LinkedIn and YouTube. I'm pretty much accessible. If people send me questions, I'm happy to answer them. I don't necessarily answer them immediately because I do have a life outside of trading, with my little ones. They definitely come first. But I do try to help people, because it really wasn't that long ago that I was in their shoes learning, trying to figure out the market, and trying to make headway with all the information. I had to process it, and figure out the best route for myself.

Jacob: Awesome. Well, thank you so much for allowing me to interview you for the Digital Stock Summit. I am really excited to share this with everybody. And as I was telling you beforehand, I am actually going to leave this interview up publicly for everybody to see for as long as the Digital Stock Summit site is live. I think it's definitely a valuable one that everybody should be able to see, so I wanted to make sure I share it with everyone. It will be under your profile page, so you can just search AirplaneJane or Jane on the website and you'll find that, as well as on YouTube and wherever Jane shares it. So, yeah, thank you so much and I guess, until next time.

Jane: Thank you, Jacob. Have a wonderful day.

Jacob: Thanks. You too.

Latoya M. Smith-Dean

USA

Instagram: Tradeandtikes
Facebook: Latoya Trading
Website: www.tradesandtikes.com

I found Latoya through her posts on Instagram. I was really intrigued to reach out to her, as I saw she was a mother trading like me. Little did I know that she started in the same way as myself, learning from Timothy Sykes. I'm sure her story will inspire you.

Jane:　　　What is your back-story in coming to trading?

Latoya:　　I started trading in I would say late 2006, early 2007. I graduated from college in 2005, and came back to Massachusetts. I stayed local but my friends went out of town and out of state. When my friends came back, they said, "Hey, let's start an investment club." I had no clue, no idea. I said, "Yeah. Sure. Whatever." It was something for us to do. So we did that.

Jane:　　　Was it a group of women who did it all together?

Latoya: No. The friend who approached me is a female. Her name is Alex. Alex approached me and said, "Hey Latoya, let's do an investment club. Let's get some like-minded people and start this." I said, "Sure." We started with our friend Michael and another guy named Craig. There were two males, me, and another female. There were four of us combined. Later on we grew to about six. But that's how I initially started. We started pooling monies together, and opened a brokerage account. We had Scottrade account at the time. I was the treasurer. I funded the account with the money and also bought the stocks that were picked once a month. Once a month we'd meet to discuss and determine what to buy, and then from there I'd place it in the account and send out an email: "Hey, we're in Walmart at X dollars per share."

It went on like that for months and months. I was with the club, I'd say about two to three years. But already within the first six months to a year I really started getting the feel of the portfolio. At that time, I worked for State Street Corp. I was able to sit and look at the computer because that was my job. It was all computer work, and I was a back-end financial analyst, so I was computing and analyzing data. I was able to watch the price movement of stocks all day. I'd say "Hey, we should sell this, we're up." But we were more long-term based. That's when I decided, "Let me open my own brokerage account," and then it was just history after that.

Jane: So it sounds like you opened up the account in 2010?

Latoya: No, I opened my brokerage account in 2007. So it was probably six months after we started the club and then

I just started to get a feel for things. From there, like any other person, I'd go online and research how to start a hedge fund, how to day trade, how to do this. Before you even know it I ran into this website. But this website is not the website you know it to be today. This website, timothysykes.com, had Tim Sykes saying he was going to replicate what he did in college. He had zero background history. It was just a blog from scratch. A guy saying, "Hey, I'm going to take 12K and turn it into some millions like I did in college." Yeah, sure, buddy. Let me see you do it.

So, within that process, I started to follow his blog because there was no one else around who was doing that or publicly listing stocks. I started following his blog and then I started getting into penny stocks, the whole concept of shorting. I tried everything. In terms of shorting, the strategy, keep in mind, he had not paid anything. It was just free information, so I was able to connect with him directly, or make commentary on his blog, and he would give me feedback. I learned a lot in that process as well and gained experience in general. Just doing it on my own, learning from my mistakes at the same time. But I really like the whole aspect of shorting a lot, so at the time he recommended "Thinkorswim". And this broker was a stand-alone. This was before TD Ameritrade bought them out. I opened an account there with them. And then, I really began shorting stocks and doing that strategy for a little bit. So that's how my process started.

In 2008 I stopped trading. I went into real estate, and ended up buying and flipping houses. I had that part of me like, "Hey! You were missing in action for all these years." It's because I started doing real estate. I stopped trading completely, and went into that, flipping houses and all that madness, and I just... Hey I'd rather do trading. It's easier. That's why I disappeared for a few years, and then I came back, and I was like, "Whoa! Tim you really made all this money?"

Jane: Basically your time frame was you started in 2006 with a group, and then opened your own account six to seven months later. Then you closed everything out in 2008?

Latoya: I just closed the day trading part, but not the IRA part. When everything dropped in '08 around that time, that's when I just... I had nothing but time to buy in stuff in the retirement account. "This looks good; this won't go bankrupt." Sirius is the only thing around after they merged with XM. Why would they let that fail? Especially... It was like 10 cents once. It's a no brainer. Certain financial stocks as well were ridiculously low. At that time it was more Roth investing. And then after I bought the house in '08 that was... Pretty much I had to pull out the day trading money, because I started buying flip houses. I needed the capital to work on the projects.

Jane: I hear you...When did you come back to the day trading world?

Latoya: I didn't come back until almost 2011, believe it or not. Some real estate agent convinced me, "Don't quit your job yet." No, I told her at that point. When I found Tim, and saw he was real, I'm like I can do this trading thing. I wanted to quit. I really did. "Well don't. Buy your house first." She didn't tell me you have to keep a job in order to pay the mortgage to buy the house. So I just went off that path for a little bit but I found my way back to my true calling.

Jane: Now just out of curiosity, what did you study in school before you went into the financial world?

Latoya: I studied business management with a concentration in finance. I was basically in finance with a BS in Finance.

Jane: And would you have called Timothy Sykes your mentor in the beginning? Or did you have anyone else that you really worked with who helped you along the way?

Latoya: He pretty much was the only person at the time that was actually out there in the internet world to follow. There was no one else, really and truly. There was no one else.

Jane: That's how I found out about day trading, intra-day trading as well, through finding his site and then using his tools to start. Then I found the strategy that worked for me.

Do you have any books that you started off with in the beginning or DVDs that you watched that you would recommend to somebody starting out today? Because it is definitely hard. There's a lot to learn. It's an ocean of knowledge to learn.

Latoya: In terms of DVDs I haven't watched a single DVD. Unfortunately, I have to say that in terms of books... I'm trying to really remember the author's name but it will come back to me probably throughout the interview. I received a lot of information through other traders that are not known. Over time I've gotten to know a lot of great traders and I've learned a lot from them. In terms of information online or, "Hey, read this book, this will help you," I'm not the one to suggest them because I haven't done it myself. I hate to say that, but it's true.

Jane: No, the main reason for this book is to help others learn from our experiences. Something that was important for me in the beginning was reading *Momo Traders* by Brady Dahl and *Market Wizards* by Jack Schwager, which are all about sharing good traders' experiences and I learned a lot from that as well.

Do you trade from home? Or do you trade on the road?

Latoya: I trade from home. I trade mainly from home. I don't travel and trade or anything like that. It's just strictly from home.

Jane: What sort of setup do you use?

Latoya: My current setup is my MacBook Pro that I use to execute my trades and I have three monitors. I have one monitor set up vertically and then two main monitors. Three monitors and a MacBook Pro.

Jane: Got it. I've got two laptops and three monitors, so I hear you with that. And what's your typical research for setting up your trading day?

Latoya: Alright. So, I'll start with CNNMoney.com, then there's also nasdaq.com, that have pre-market movers. I look for volatility. I trade gaps, specifically. So, I'm a gap trader. And then also, on my platform "Think or Swim", there's a market watch where you can go through the little tabs "Lovers and Losers", and then you can also find after hours as well as pre-market data. I take all of those stocks, but they have to be volume related, and that's how I construct my watch list.

Jane: Okay, do you have a minimum for volume that you're going to look at for a gapper, either direction?

Latoya: Over time I've learned that I can't eliminate just because I only see, let's say, 20,000 shares traded or 10,000 shares. Because what I've come to realize, let's say during the trading day, the same one I did not put on my list is the same one that performed very well, just because it had a lack of volume in pre-market. I really like the ones with, I'll say at least 50,000 in volume in pre-market to start. But I will still have those that, let's say have 20k or 10k in volume in pre-market. I'll throw them on the side so I can keep a watch. But the ones with heavier volume, I'll focus on, and I'll have them on my main screen.

Jane: And how many do you typically have when you start out your day that are on your watch list?

Latoya: For me, I try to narrow it down to no more than six stocks. No more than that. And it's different when I moderate. When you moderate, there are a lot of people who say, "Hey look at this, look at that." So the list could be 18, 20 stocks long. But realistically, yes on that screen, "Hey I'm watching it for you guys", but on my screen I'm really focused on "Hey, this is what I'm trading today." So for me personally, no more than six.

Jane: Okay. And what time do you typically start your trading day?

Latoya: About 8:15 am Eastern Time.

Jane: Do you have any other specific software or scanning tools that you use?

Latoya: I do not. Besides thinkorswim, I do not. All the websites out there pull the same information, unless you're a particular trader. If you look for small caps, penny caps, I believe software is definitely needed because not all the major websites will have those. So, it depends on your specialty.

Jane: Now you mentioned that you're a moderator as well. In the chat room (Real Life Trading)... Do you use Trading View as well for your charting software?

Latoya: I use it only with the trading room, but it's very nice actually. I like it. I like the part where you can control it with your mouse, especially if you have a Mac. You can control it with your fingers, and zoom in and zoom out really easily. It's very user-friendly so I like that software. I've started implementing it now. But before it was just strictly Thinkorswim, because I love it.

Jane: It's the same for me. I'm a creature of habit. You get used to a certain platform and you get used to using it, and it's hard to switch because you're used to it day-to-day.

Latoya: Yes.

Jane: Now, you said before that you learned shorting from Timothy Sykes. You feel that you're more of a gap trader, but are you more preferential towards shorts?

Latoya: Yes, I'm short 95% of the time. My eyes are trained to see the setups. If I see a gap list, I'm looking at the gap downs first before I even consider the gap ups. Because gap downs are going to go further down. That's how

I perceive it. So, yes, I'm short bias. And yes, it is due to him.

Jane: Not a bad thing. Now, it's interesting that you like to short gap down stocks whereas I tend to trade the reversals on them. I tend to trade the reversal bounces when the shorts are getting squeezed.

Latoya: Interesting. There's a method to the madness just through back testing alone. That's why usually when I trade, I'm done by 10:00, 10:15. So just think about that. If they're going to go down they're going down for the straight 30 minutes, right? I'm out, I'm gone. You're going to catch the reversals, after 10:15, 10:30, and it bounces up.

Jane: Exactly. And then there's the 10:30 fakeout where it bounces and then it continues down, but I hear you 100%. Now, when you're trading, do you tend to go all in at the beginning, or do you scale in and out of trades?

Latoya: It depends on the trade. It really depends on the trade. Some trades, I feel comfortable, and I'll go all in. And then other trades I'm like, "Eh." I don't trust them so I'll just start scaling in. And then I really want to see that morning high first and that usually happens within the first three minutes of the market. You get that spike. Bam, that's my high. This is my low, and then we'll go from there. So that's how I generally work things. And then once it breaks a certain low, I'm adding like crazy because it's going to drop. So that's how I initially trade.

Jane: My next question is do you add to losers or winners? But you're adding to your winners, it sounds like, once you hit a certain support break.

If it starts going against you, are you going to go ahead and use a hard stop or mental stop and get out, or will you let it go so far and then potentially add because you're confident that it's going to, in your scenario, shorting continue down?

Latoya: Alright. Usually when I'm in a trade, I have a mental stop, and the mental stop is normally a few pennies above the high that the stock put in in the morning. I'm willing to let it go against me. If I'm not in full position, then I start adding. As long as it doesn't breach that mental stop, I'm still in the trade. If it reverses and goes my way, I'll just slap on some more shares and then that's it for that trade. But let's say if something goes against me, hits my mental stop, I'm out. And you'll find that through moderating, I actually use physical stops because that's the way they run the room. There's a stop, target, entry. It's very structured and specific, so I obey it. If I'm trading on my own, I don't use hard stops because I realize hard stops take you right out. Because everyone's thinking pretty much the same. They place the stops at the very same place.

Jane: I also find that hard stops tend to get sold to the market makers by the brokers, and will get executed. Market makers will manipulate it to go ahead and have that transaction get filled.

Latoya: Yes, definitely.

Jane: Now, how many stocks will you typically trade at one time? Are you usually just watching one, or will you be up to five? How many do you tend to trade?

Latoya: No more than two. No more than two stocks, that's it. Because usually I go full position. If I'm full position, I can't focus on any other one anyways. There's no capital left. I'm full position in this trade, and that's it. If I focus on one, it more than likely works out. There will be no need to trade anything else. I close it down for the day; that's it.

Jane: I know you usually say you're done by 10:15 am. Do you tend to ever hold a swing trade overnight, or are you strictly intraday?

Latoya: No, I don't hold anything if it's not in my plan. If I have not done analysis on that stock prior, or if it's not at a certain level, there's no reason for me to hold the stock overnight. If I'm in something as a day trade, that's it. I'll give it a certain amount of time. Or if it looks like it will have a late breakdown, then I'll sit there a little while until it breaks down, but no swing positions. And another thing I wanted to mention is 10:15 am is no longer... I find that throughout, I would say about seven months now, the market has changed a little bit, so instead of things breaking down immediately, they're taking a little bit longer now. So I'm sitting there a little bit longer; I'm sitting there till 11:00 am or 11:15 am. So it's not really 10:15 am anymore. Once the market changes you have to adapt to that change and realize that this is not performing the way it used to.

Jane: Definitely. Now, as far as your risk management, with your position sizing, do you have a set amount that you're willing to risk for the day or for the trade, or a dollar amount that you're looking at when it comes to your risk management?

Latoya: In terms of risk management I always aim for 3:1, 2:1. Most of the time I can get by with 6:1. It really depends on the trade. But in terms of actual dollar amount, I'm not willing to lose more than 300 bucks for the day; that's it. Three hundred dollars - I cut it off, and I stay within those means. But I also have rules to prevent a $300 loss. For example, I can't make more than three day trades. If the first day trade's a loser, and it's almost $300, I cut it off. It doesn't matter. So I have little rules in place to prevent that from happening.

Jane: Okay, what are your rules? I'll go ahead and ask you, do you have a list? I actually have a list that I have at my desk.

Latoya: Nice, nice. Oh wow.

Jane: Just to remind me because the visual helps to remind me day-to-day.

Latoya: Nice. Mine are more embedded in my mind. I have them written out in several notebooks but it's never on the desk, in my face or anything. I just know I can't trade more than three times for the day. Three day trades, that's it. The fourth one is just normally a bonus. It's just a bonus. But at three, I stop. I'm not supposed to trade past 12:00 pm, period. That's time for my kids, to let them do whatever they need to do. And that's generally all the patience I have as well. I can't trade the first two to three minutes of the market. That's also part of my rules. I don't just dive right in. I sit back and wait for the two minute bars to set up. I have rules in terms of share size. So if I'm in at a thousand shares, what is my risk tolerance there? A thousand shares, 30 cents stop would be a $300 loss. And that's how I trade.

Jane: Okay, great. It sounds like you're really good at mitigating risks so that you have small losses. Do you remember your biggest loss?

Latoya: Yes, $5,000.

Jane: What was that?

Latoya: $5,000, I lost on triple D. DDD. This is way back; I don't really remember the year, but I remember the loss. The stock gapped down.

Jane: Was that early in your career or more recently?

Latoya: No, it was early on. It was not recent. No way I'm taking a 5k loss today. But this was earlier on and I was just adjusting my mind to actually day trading versus swing trading. When I was working I was able to do day trades, but most of the time, it would be swing trades. I'm in it for one to two, three days and it worked that way. But just transitioning to a day trader and not really understanding the market dynamics can get you into trouble. At the time, I didn't really understand the market dynamics, and hey, this is just going to go down. And it is more of revenge trading after I lost a grand and then I just kept going back at the same stock and then, 5k gone just like that in one day. Nothing I could do besides learn from it.

Jane: How do you think that you recovered from that? What did you do to help yourself recover from that big loss at that time, do you remember?

Latoya: Wow! How did I recover from that loss? I believe I did not take the few days off which is always suggested. You have to step back, and take a few days off. Instead, I tried again the next day. I was just really inexperienced at the time, to be honest with you. So to say I've learned from that loss; yes, today, in my mind, yes I have. But then looking back, I still kept on trading. So no, back then, I did not learn from the loss. That was my biggest loss. 5k in one day.

Jane: My biggest losing trade was 9k, but that was a swing trade that I was bag holding and it was not good. Now how about the flip side: what was your biggest win?

Latoya: Wow! There have been a lot. In terms of day trading win, my biggest win would have been $62,000 on a day trade.

Jane: And what sort of capital did it take to gain the $62,000 for you? What was the return I should say?

Latoya: Oh, it was off of a $50,000 capital. At the time, it was FNMA, Fannie Mae. It was that stock that went crazy. But I didn't really risk a lot in turn because of the actual price. It was a dollar something and it went to almost $5. But I got out way before... I could've made so much more, but I got out way before the actual $4 something hit. So, that was the biggest one I had in terms of a day trade. Or I think it took two days for it to get there. I have long term investments that have actually made more, such as Tesla. I had Tesla at like $40 something sold at $200. That was in my Roth with SIRI, at 34 cents average, and I sold that to. That got to $4 and change. So I have some heavy hitters in my long term account.

Jane: Those are all great. Do you use your Level 2 when you're trading, or are you strictly trading the charts? And if you're trading just the charts, do you use indicators?

Latoya: Alright, so Level 2. I find that Level 2 is not great for large caps. I tend to trade large caps. I shouldn't say large caps because it also depends on the market cap. Let's say shares are $30 and up to $100. $100 is my cap price for stocks, with the exception of Netflix or Apple. But you can't use Level 2 for those because I find that they're not always accurate. You'll see a lot of things in a book: all of a sudden, they disappear. They're no longer there. Hey, what happened to that... It's gone? Or my broker, besides thinkorswim, I also execute day trades with Lightspeed Trader. Lightspeed Trader, I can hide my position. I can hide my share size so you will not see it show up on Level 2. And I understand a lot of traders do that, especially if you work for a prop firm or something like that. So I don't use Level 2 in terms of that, but the only time I use Level 2 is if something gets to a whole number, like a 28. Then all of a sudden, I see that they start stacking up a bit. Now I'm watching time and sales to see what's really happening. Do they want to break it, or do they want to bounce off of it as support? So that's the only time I'll use Level 2, but it's mainly price action that I use. And in terms of indicators, moving averages are really the only things that are on my charts, that's it.

Jane: Which ones do you use for moving averages?

Latoya: I use the nine, the 20, the 50, and the 200. I use them for daily time frames, so they'll stick on a chart if I change the time frame one minute, five minute, 10 minutes, 15 minutes. I use different time frames back and forth depending on the day, but the MAs work pretty great as well as the VWAP, volume-weighted price action.

Jane: As far as being a female in the trading world, do you see any big hurdles for women getting into the trading world?

Latoya: Wow! I never actually thought about it like that in terms of being a woman. The number one thing is to really have an interest in trading, because you have to be extremely passionate about it. A lot of people will look at it and they won't have the passion for trading or probably they don't understand it. It's really something where you have to have passion for it. I believe no matter who you are, it shouldn't matter. If you have the passion, it should not hinder your ability to perform well in the stock market. That's one thing about the market; it has no biases, zero. The markets don't care who you are; they will take your money.

Jane: Absolutely, and that's what I like to say too. It doesn't matter who's behind the computer screen. Man or Woman: you are just a person, and it's you against the market. That's it! Now, do you have any advice for any new traders, particularly female traders?

Latoya: Yes. I would definitely suggest, even before trading real money, try to get as much information as you possibly can. Access all the information they have out there, whether it's books or videos, or let's say you go online, you could find a reputable mentor. When I mentor people, I recommend you get as much knowledge as possible before you even risk your real money. And then I advise you to paper trade first. To put everything you've learned from whomever, put that to test using paper money and treat it like it's real money so you can get the hang of it. And then from there, if you're consistent in a paper account with a reputable strategy and real rules, then you can proceed to actually opening a brokerage account, and risking real money. But I would say go that step first. I wish I'd done that first.

I was so eager and hungry at the same time that I went straight ahead with real money, not thinking the world of anything, and I'll tell you why. That's what happens when you have a clutch. My clutch was my nine-to-five. I made great money. And when you have a clutch like that and you're trading, it's like, "Ah, I lost this. Ugh." You're just funding the account, because what else you going to do? You don't really have a motive to be serious. I feel like the seriousness kicks in once you don't have that clutch anymore. Once you become a trader, you think, "Hey, this is my income. I have no choice. I have to rely on this." And that's pretty much what I will suggest to new traders: just get educated first, paper trade next, and then proceed.

Jane: I agree 100%. Now when you started out, did you ever use anything to analyze your trades in the beginning to see that your winning ratio was greater than 50:50, which is basically the odds when you go in?

Latoya: In the beginning, no. I just based it off of my brokerage account at the end of the year. So I'm either green or it's just like, "Hey, I just wasted my time and just lost XYZ." That's how I used to base it in the past, but now I actually have an actual spreadsheet that tracks my wins, my losses, and everything to see that nice percentage ratio.

Jane: Do you update that daily, or do you update that weekly?

Latoya: I try to update it daily.

Jane: Well if you're doing three trades, it's easy. Right?

Latoya: Oh, yeah. But sometimes I only trade once... If you visit the chat room, you'll see I made one trade and that's it. That trade's a winner, and that's it; there's nothing else.

What else should I do? That's it. And it's so funny, 'cause I'm on Instagram a lot, and I used to post a lot of the trades. I used to post my profits and losses. And they would ask me, "You don't have any losses? Where are your losses?" If you understand, sometimes I only make one trade. One trade, that's it. You get losses when you overtrade.

Jane: Now as a woman, we have our real life that interacts with trading. How do you balance your trading life and your home life? Because I know you have two kids, so how is that balanced for you as a female in the trading world?

Latoya: Might be a little hard for me to explain because when I actually did become a full-time day trader, this is when my first child was born. She was born in 2013, so 2012 is when I left my full-time job. She was my trading partner. I used to have the bottle on my desk: I'm feeding and I'm trading. When I put her to sleep, she was right there in her bassinet next to me. I'm on the bed trading and at that time I only used to trade off of my MacBook, that was it. I was that programmed, with one screen, and it was like that for almost two years. Then my second was born, and it was the same way. Not a big adjustment, but I adapted as one was walking, potty training, getting up, going back and forth. I just made sure that if I had to leave the platform that I was not in the trade. So that helped a lot. I just made sure their needs were met first. Currently I do breakfast in the morning, about 7:45 am, by 8:00 am they are fed, they have their snacks, they have their juice, and I'm trading with them in the same room. They're right there with me. They have all their toys, we have a TV, they have DVDs.

Jane: Aww.

Latoya: So they're entertained for a few hours. That's why it's very important for me to cut it off at 12:00 pm because it's not in my interest nor theirs for me to feel like I'm neglecting them. Because that defeats the purpose of me becoming a day trader. It's really so I can be there for them, watch them grow; that's why they are with me every single day.

Jane: I hear you 100% and I applaud you on that because I couldn't do it when my daughter was home. I had to wait until she was at daycare before I could really get into it full-time, so we shall see how it is with the second one. And now that you have your two kids, do you travel at all while you're trading? I think you said no you don't travel and trade.

Latoya: No, I don't travel and trade, so if we go on vacation we are gone. The computer stays home. I don't care what's happening in the market; when I come back, okay, then it's trading time again. But when I'm on vacation I don't think about the markets. I'm swimming, I'm on the beach, I'm enjoying life, and I'm not the one to trade abroad or something like that. Not at all.

Jane: Have you seen that your success in trading has caused any difficulties in your personal relationships?

Latoya: In the beginning, this is even before I had kids so I've been with my husband for, what's that? Since 2006? What's that, 10 years? Wow!

Jane: Congratulations.

Latoya: We haven't been married for 10 years but we have been together that long. But in the beginning, yeah, he didn't like the idea of trading. He didn't like the financial markets, the fact that people can make so much money on a computer. What are they providing to society? Trust me, I had that conversation many times, but when I actually started doing it and producing results, all that just went out the window. Just like, "Hey, how's your day going today?" It just feels great. So that's no longer an issue. It's not an issue, it's not a big deal, so no, it hasn't hindered any relationships at all.

Jane: That's great; that's wonderful. Now as you were saying, your profits started to roll in and everything was good with that. How long would you say it took you as a trader to feel like you were successful in the day trading? And was it an overall profit amount that you were looking for, or was it just being consistent?

Latoya: It was being consistent. It had nothing to do with the money because one day, let's say inexperienced Latoya back then could make 10k in a given week, and then the next week I could lose $15,000. I would lose not only the $10,000 I had made, but I would also lose part of the capital. So that's inconsistent. It would have nothing to do with the amount of money. So when I started seeing consistency, that was letting me know that oh, I'm getting somewhere. Because eventually you're consistent. The money comes, the money adds up, so it's more being consistent than the actual money.

Jane: And how long was it until you were feeling like the consistency was there for you?

Latoya: I'd say it took about seven months. I had to reconstruct. I had to do a few things. I had to backtrack, and then from there, once I'd done all of that, I had to construct my rules to say, you know what? What I've done in the past was just crazy. It's just, I don't even know how to explain it. I had too much money in my account, number one. So that was initially a problem. Once I cut that in half, and then just started really trading around rules, and becoming more robotic, then I just started seeing consistency. I knew the strategy I had definitely worked.

Jane: And would you say you find it hard to be robotic, and take the emotions out of trading?

Latoya: No. Not anymore, not anymore. I'm very, very meticulous, very. I trade around a certain time every day. I don't trade before a certain time every day. I'm out of the trade... I take my profit in partials as well. I'll take the majority off once it hits a certain target, and the rest will just... I'll let it ride free. And just put a physical stop at that point, and let it hit. I'm still profitable. I'm just very structured within my trading day.

Jane: Is there anything else that we didn't cover that you would like to share to newer traders, or anyone just entering the trading world?

Latoya: I would say... Take time out to discover who you are as a trader. Just because one method may work for somebody else that doesn't mean it will work for you. For example, although in the beginning I learned about penny stocks back in 2007, and watching Tim do his thing, I initially found that me trading a certain price range is not for me. I developed my own strategy and just started sticking to particular stocks that I felt comfortable trading. Once you take your time to find out the person you are, and the type of trader you want to be, then you can proceed from there. Don't be afraid to dabble in different markets. For example, Futures is a great market besides stocks. Some may like Forex. So really dabble before you say, "Hey, you know what? I want to trade this market, or that market." Just find yourself first as a trader. On my website I mentor beginners. I also mentor advanced traders, and those that are looking for a strategy. I'll teach my strategy with no problem.

Jane: And you're also moderating twice a week, right?

Latoya: Yes, I moderate twice a week for Real Life Trading on Mondays and Thursdays.

Jane: Thank you, Latoya, thank you very much. Actually I have the link, so I'm going to see if I can pop in the room tomorrow morning. I've got a busy, busy day ahead, but I'm going try and come and visit with you guys again tomorrow morning.

Latoya: Alright, thank you, have a great night.

Jane: Thanks, you too.

Sarah Potter

Canada

Website: Shecantrade.com
Twitter: @shecantrade
YouTube: She CanTrade
Book: *How You Can Trade Like a Pro*

Sarah was a referred to me by Stephanie Kammerman, another trader featured in this book. Once we began speaking, I learned she is primarily a trader of options. She has proven that the strategies you can develop can be used across different markets. When Sarah began trading she started a blog that eventually blossomed into a training program and a book written from a former teacher's standpoint.

Jane: What brought you to trading for a career?

Sarah: Well, I dabbled in trading way back. I think everyone has these sorts of stories. It was back in high school in economics class, and I decided to do this newspaper trading stock challenge. I was kind of intrigued by it. Of course, I didn't make any money and I didn't win the competition, but I really started getting excited about trading. Then I always just wanted to dabble in it, and one day I decided, "Yeah, I'm going to start trying to figure all this out," and I did. So I don't really have a moment in time where I can say it was exactly this date. Certainly I've always been interested in it and always kind of kept coming back to try it.

Jane: Obviously that was high school, right? So did you go through college, and then you went into a career, and you did it on the side as well?

Sarah: Yes, I started in high school, then went to university, tried a different career, just didn't really think about it for a few years. Then I started trading during that whole tech boom. I had the idea of, "Oh, I'm just going to buy some stocks," and just kind of worked it in then. Everyone was buying Nortel in Canada, so that was pretty exciting at the time. But again, I wasn't really trying to do it full-time. I never really thought I could do it full-time at that point, and it wasn't until I was further along in my career, and probably about 10 years ago now, that I really started to say, "This would be a really great way to earn a living." I didn't know if this is possible, but I was going try it. I was going to try. I was still working full-time when I started to do this on the side. I tried different strategies, and started in futures and did that for a little bit, but really found that options were a lot more of my style. They really allowed me to trade and still work. So that's really when I started honing in on my skills and finding some setups and trades that really worked well for me. I then made the switch and have never looked back. It's the absolute best career in the whole world, and I hope that other people can do the same thing because it's pretty great to be able to work from home and have a nice balanced lifestyle and still be able to earn a living.

Jane: Now what was your career at the time about 10 years ago when you said you really got into it with your options trading? Was that in the financial world at all, or was it completely different?

Sarah: Not at all. I was in education. I was a consultant. I would do professional development for people. I basically took the information I knew about teaching and learning and I applied it to myself in terms of learning a new skill, which was trading. That's how I bridged the gap. When I first started trading, I knew nothing. I didn't know what a call and a put was, so I had a long journey, and that's why I am a big advocate of "Anybody can do this." If I can do this, anyone can do it. It is just a matter of understanding that it's a skill set to be learned, and just like anything else, it takes time to learn it, but everybody can get here.

Jane: **I agree 100%.** Now when you first got interested and started your journey 10 years ago, did you have a mentor who helped you along your way? Was there anyone who helped you when you didn't know what the terms were or anything like that?

Sarah: No. I was searching for that and I was actually quite disappointed in the industry, because I couldn't really find anybody who I could trust. I wanted to find someone who would be reliable to be able to ask some good questions and get some real answers. That's why I started the blog shecantrade.com, and way back then it was just a blog, because I was frustrated. There weren't people out there who were really answering questions in a very direct and authentic way. I thought there was a lot of marketing out there and I didn't like that. So I had to do a lot of stuff on my own. There was a lot of trial and error, and just a lot of random research. I didn't have one site or one person that really was instrumental. I looked and tried, but I could never find somebody. That's a big reason why I wrote my book and why I did what I did because I wanted to be that for other people. I wanted to be able to break down this industry in a way that we can talk about it, that people can understand, and that it's something that you can do responsibly.

Jane: I agree 100%. It's funny to hear you say that, because that's basically where the idea for this book came about. I was looking for female trading mentors and not really seeing very many women online. Like you, I also ended up sharing my trading story on my blog too. It's interesting that we both have that background to want to share. I'm not sure if it's a female thing or if it's just we saw a need for it and so we're trying to fill the need.

Sarah: Yes. So for me, She Can Trade was really more about... I guess it sounds funny, but I was frustrated because I thought, "Wow, I can really do this." So I came up with the message, the URL, shecantrade.com. But a lot of people, I've now realized, read the URL and think that I'm only talking about women, but I'm not. I was and am trying to help everybody.

Jane: I understand.

Sarah: But you know what? I think you're right. I think maybe women have more of a nature of wanting to help other people and not feeling insecure. There's nothing wrong with all of us helping everybody so that we can all do well. The market's huge. Of all places, it's huge. There's enough room for everybody to do well in the market. That's the best reason to share something, and that's why I wrote my book. *How You Can Trade Like a Pro* came about that way as well. That's what the book is all about. It's breaking things down in a way that is simple and straightforward for people to understand. Whether you want to trade for yourself or you want to be a little bit more informed in order to ask better questions of your investment advisor, I think a little information can go a long way. So in my book I take a lot of complicated terms and setups and really simplify it. I give people some real setups, like systems: "Step one, two, three, four, five. Do this," in terms of trade setups and then how to actually gather evidence in a very repeatable and consistent approach to trading.

Jane: So when you started do you remember three books or tools that you would recommend for beginning traders? Yours, in itself, is a great beginning tool, but is there anything else that you might recommend for someone? Obviously it's a different market now and different information is out there. But was there anything that you started with that really stuck out in your mind as informative in the beginning?

Sarah: When I look back at the books that helped me the most, the books that I found most helpful were not trading books at all. I actually think there are a lot of trading books out there that really don't explain anything in our industry. I'm sure you can relate; our industry suffers from the same people explaining the same things the same way.

Jane: I am just now learning options, so it is new to me.

Sarah: Okay, so you're probably in this right now. If you go on Google options trading, it's the same symbol. Someone will say, "Oh, yeah, I'm going to trade a strangle," and then it's this line graph and everybody shows the exact same thing. When I was first learning, I always thought, "Do people not really know what they're talking about because how come no one can explain it any other way other than this?" Because that didn't make sense to me at all. So I actually found trading books very frustrating. Instead, I found other more motivational books to be quite helpful. *Drive* by Daniel H. Pink and *Mindset* by Carol S. Dweck are about how to tackle problems and how to overcome problems. I found those a lot more helpful than any technical analysis book or options 101 books. It's that balance when you're learning that is so important. I'll put on my education consultant hat for a moment: when you're learning a new skill, there's a balance between having to sort through the information and understanding it, but also, it needs to be applicable. When you're trading, just like whatever instrument you're using, it's one thing just to read a book and have the knowledge of what a call is or what a put is, but you have to be able to put that together to actually do something with it. I found that a lot of books didn't actually take that part across; they didn't take it from what a definition is to "Well, what does it actually look like and what do you do with it?" So that's why I wrote my book in the way that I wrote it. I thought it needs to be more useful. "How do I actually do stuff in the market?" Yeah, does that answer your question, or have I segued...

Jane: No, that definitely answers my question because it is important to understand the why behind something instead of "It is what it is." I think that's also something that women potentially bring to the table as we look at it from a different perspective. It's like when you ask a man to give directions and you ask a woman to give directions. Women tend to give you landmarks and men tend to give you distance measurements. It's just an interesting way that the minds work differently, and bringing your explanation of the why behind it can help enlighten people as to the bigger picture instead of just "Memorize this chart."

Sarah: Yeah, exactly. Go repeat that. Yeah, I think that's actually a perfect example. Mapping is a great way. So, if you're learning how to trade, think of that analogy. If I asked a friend of mine how to get to a new gas station, how would they describe the route? Because people will all use different tools, but everyone will end up at the same gas station. Some people use GPS, some people will use a visual map, other people will want to see words written down in terms of instructions, or step-by-step written words. Everybody needs to do it a little differently, but we'll all end up at the same gas station. One wife might get mad at a husband because he's not listening, but we will all get there. And it's kind of the same thing with trading. So if you are learning, I think it's important that you're learning from someone who has a similar trading personality as you so that it does match your style or your learning style, and that way you'll excel at trading a lot faster.

Jane: And that's why I always recommend people to paper trade, to try and find the strategy that applies to them, because our trading strategy is like a fingerprint. Everybody is different in terms of risk tolerance, what they deal with, and their time limit that they can devote to the trade. Therefore different trading styles work for different people and you just have to figure that out. So now you're at home, you have two girls, what do you use for your trading setup?

Sarah: I don't really have one and I don't think you need a fancy trade setup. So I just trade from a regular computer with two monitors. I actually like to spend the winters in California. When I'm there trading, I'm just trading from a laptop with one external monitor.

Jane: Very nice.

Sarah: So you really don't need anything fancy. And I am also known to pull over in a parking lot and check my phone and check positions. I'm definitely utilizing my cell phone a lot because you can't always... You don't always have time to be able to pull up all the screens and look at it. Sometimes it's just a matter of monitoring things on my phone and I do that a lot.

Jane: Definitely. Now do you still dabble in futures as well, or is it just options that you're trading now?

Sarah: Well I'm always changing depending on how the market's moving and where the best trades are found. I never stopped trading options because honestly, of all the tools out there, I think that is the best way to be leveraged, to be safe, and to still be able to do something else without being stuck in front of the computer screen all the time. So for me, it is a huge bias. However, there are still trades to be had in futures, especially options on futures; those are also really great. And then I will dabble in stocks as well, but my main paycheck, if you will, is options.

Jane: You have your two girls, so how do you typically have your day set up, and what do you do to research for your trading day?

Sarah: My trading style is swing trading. I have made a rule for myself, and this was prior to having children: I don't ever trade on Mondays. I feel like we work so hard to be able to have the ability to do other things other than trade, and this lifestyle allows you to do that. I thought, "You know what? I'm always going to have a three-day weekend." So I always have that extra day, and being that my girls are quite young, it's nice because I honor that day, that's their day, and we have fun together. I do spend some time on Mondays, though I don't trade, but I will sit down for at least half an hour and just go through stocks, just kind of get a feel or a pulse of what's happening, because I like to see how things are setting up that week. But I never put the pressure on myself to actually place a trade. That's been very helpful for me, for one. And then the rest of the week, what I do is... My favorite time to trade is between 11am to 12 pm Eastern Time, so I try to keep that time honored as trading time. I will pay attention to how the market opens in the morning, and then I will step away from it, generally for about half an hour. Then they'll start ramping up into 11, and then 11 to 12 is my trading time. I will not check the markets, generally, for lunch, and then I'll come back around 2:30 and try to check-in.

Jane: Okay.

Sarah: And I also swing-trade, so I hold trades usually about three to five days. So there's nothing that I get into one day, that I would really need to get out of that day. Usually I'm just letting the profit run there. That trading style allows me to still have time to do other things. When I had my first daughter, I still trained for a marathon. I still had other things I could go do as well because the style, the approach to trading that way, still allows you to do other things while trading.

Jane: For sure.

Sarah: It took a while and it was difficult to learn what trade setups I could actually work with. That's why I don't trade as many futures now, because with futures trading, you do have to be in front of the computer screen waiting for that setup to occur. Sometimes that can take up a lot more time in front of the computer, which takes away from other things.

Jane: I understand completely. So what would you say is the strategy, besides being a swing-trader, that you use with your options to help you be able to do them as swing-trades?

Sarah: So my two favorite trades of all times are credit spreads, and trading those out of the money, and then buying calls and puts. Now the level I'm going to pick or the length of time I'm going to trade is going to depend on how the market's moving. At the essential core of it all, you don't have to get complicated in options. I know options... The downfall to options is that there are so many different types of strategies to trade, and so many ways to add on legs, take off legs, roll trades, et cetera, that I think sometimes people think it needs to be really complicated to be very effective. But my approach is very effective and very simple and clean; just straightforward trading.

Jane: Now do you ever hedge? Do you ever hedge with a put and a call, and you will close-out the swing depending on which one's in the profit, or do you just typically go just one put or one call?

Sarah: Yes. Typically I will spend a lot of time upfront for trades. I try to say I put the work into the trade before I put my money down because I don't roll trades; I don't generally need to. I just focus on putting the work in right from the beginning, and so I generally will have a bias of the direction I think the market's going and I will place that trade. Now if I look at a stock, let's say, and I think it's moving sideways, then I have strategies that I'll use for a sideways move. But I'm rarely going to trade something moving sideways. Buying a strangle is not something I would do, so that idea of buying a call and put, and not knowing what direction it would go but trying to take advantage of a bigger move, based on that strategy generally I won't trade it. If something's moving sideways, I might sell a straddle or do an iron condor maybe, depending on how things are moving of course. Generally I will have a bias about which direction I think that one's going and I'll trade in that direction.

Jane: Okay. Since you do the swing-trading, do you typically look out for the monthlies, or are you trading weeklies on the options? I know you say it depends on the market, which is obviously true, but do you look at stocks that, per se, have gapped down big time and you're looking for a reversal? Or is there a typical style of stock that you're looking for that you want for a swing-trade and also time on the option?

Sarah: Weekly options are my favorite. The way I want to trade a weekly option is obviously taking advantage of the fact that it expires within the week, but I won't necessarily trade it with that same week expiry. Let's say for a call or put, I'm going about three weeks out right now for expiry.

Jane: Are you looking more into what the general trend of the market is?

Sarah: Yes. The highest probability trades are always going to be trading in the direction where the overall trend is. That is... Time and time again, and that is me testing trade strategies for years, you are going have higher success when you're trying to trade in the same direction that something's already moving because it's more likely that it is going to have a bigger move in that direction. While sometimes I will counter-trend trade, most of the time I will be in the same direction as the trend that comes from a daily or a weekly chart. And ideally, things are lining up for me on both a weekly and daily chart. Let's say everything is moving up, then I'm going to buy a call, and what I'll do is look for a shorter term chart, like a five-minute chart. I look for the price to pull back, and then I'm going trade in the same direction as the overall trend. That just works. I know sometimes it can be kind of a little more exciting to do counter-trend trading, especially when you're sure of something that'll move fast. However, there is not as high of a probability. For me, I'd rather wait for things to pull back and then watch them go. And then, in terms of actual stocks that I will buy... I'm in high beta stocks, and that's why I'm trading the options on them as opposed to just buying the stock.

Right now I'm in Facebook, I'm in Amazon, I'm in Starbucks, I have liked Microsoft. Pretty much companies that you can recognize. I generally stay away from pharmaceuticals, and I generally stay away from stocks that are too cheap because they don't move. If something doesn't move, then I can't make money off of it.

Jane: Well it is a great way, like you were saying, to leverage your money for a higher priced stock so you can get the action without having that overall investment of buying a share at $700, for example.

Sarah: Exactly!

Jane: Now when you're doing your swing trades, how many options or calls do you tend to be in at once?

Sarah: Within the week, I'll be getting in and out of trades pretty well every day, just because they're all on a rolling cycle. Every day I'm going to probably trade at least one trade, Tuesday to Friday. So I probably end about six trades a week. Again, that's going to depend on the market sentiment. I think I only have four trades on right now because it's just lower volume. (Week before Christmas)

Jane: That makes sense.

Sarah: But on a regular week, it'd be about six to eight probably.

Jane: And do you tend to hold them over the weekend, or will you try to be in cash on Friday, and then just start fresh again on Tuesday?

Sarah: Yes, it's the goal to be all cash over the weekend, and that's what I do most of the time. But one thing that I don't like to do is I will never hold... Or most of the time I will not hold an options trade into the last week of expiry. So I'll get out of those before they expire. A lot of times, the way that I trade is I want to set the trade up so it actually will hit the profit target within 24 hours, and then if it doesn't, I generally need to hold it for a couple of days. But most of the time, I have placed a trade and set it up so that if it doesn't work, I can hold it for about three weeks. Most of the time, it's 24 to 48 hours that I'm actually in it and I've hit the profit target and moved on to the next trade.

Jane: Perfect. And what is your typical profit target? Are you looking for 25%, 30% of your initial investment, or is it a specific price on the chart?

Sarah: That all changes. That's a hard one to answer because for me, it depends on how the market's moving, and then how a stock is behaving. Because a lot of times I like to trade very similar stocks, I usually look for 10-30% profit. You've got to get used to how a stock moves, and then you get comfortable with how much to look for.

Jane: I understand. They have their own personalities.

Sarah: When I was first starting out, I would trade MasterCard and...thanks to MasterCard, it grew my account quite a bit. When I first started, I spent a lot of time really just getting to know how that stock behaves, how that option expires on Friday. Where does the premium start decaying? Things like that. I just picked it apart, and then started getting really good about that. So the range of what I'm looking for profit will depend on the average true range that you're seeing. So I want to leave the profit target just under what the average true range is. Obviously that number's changing all the time, so that's kind of the number one piece. And then also just thinking about timing, so if I make $100 overnight, in less than 24 hours, I'm probably just taking it off because that's great. And then on average, I'm buying options that aren't really any more expensive than about $4, so if I've made $100 off $400 in 24 hours, I think it'd be silly for me to keep it any longer. That's a great return.

Jane: Of course.

Sarah: My goal is always to grow my account by 5% a week. I should preface that by also saying I don't want new people to start with that. At the beginning, I think that this is the goal they should work toward. My goal has come from trading a long time and from building that skill set. Anyone can get there, but at the beginning, you need to get good at applying the trade setups and the entries and knowing how to manage and how to keep losses small. That's so important. If a trade doesn't work, just cut it loose. I'm not a financial advisor, but for me, with my own trading, what I have learned the most and what's been so important is if a trade's not working and you have a small loss, just get out of the trade because it's easier to go find another good trade than it is to keep throwing money at a problem trade. Then you're just tying up your margin in a stock that isn't doing what you thought it was doing and you were wrong about the assumption. I like to just keep them short, small, and then I just move on to all the ones that are working. And that also builds self-confidence very quickly too, and that is just so key in trading, especially for women.

Jane: One of the big things that I mention about paper trading is to build confidence and consistency so that you can find that strategy that will really work, instead of throwing away your hard-earned money in the beginning when you need to really learn the whole process.

Sarah: Absolutely. The piece I would add to that about paper is if you're trading with paper, make sure you're trading with the same amount of paper money that you are planning on trading with for real money. It's not helpful to trade a paper account at $200,000 if you're only going trade with $50,000 because your risk/reward is all out of whack. So the paper account should be very similar. That's when you're testing your strategies and you're figuring out which one works, and you're comparing them to see which one is best in terms of the amount of margin you're going have to use to place your trades. See where you get your best bang for your buck.

Jane: From what I've seen with options, there's not really a way to put in a stop like a stop limit with stocks. Is that what you mean when you're watching your stock throughout the day? Maybe you pull over to the parking lot, do you look? Are you checking to see your trades, to see if they're going against you at all, and if you want to go ahead and cut them?

Sarah: Yes, or the opposite. A lot of times, I'm like, "Oh, man! That worked, so I've got to exit out of that. I'm going to take the money."

Jane: Right.

Sarah: Just making sure that it's not too big of a loss because if it's a stock that isn't working if I am in the trade and it hasn't done what I thought it was going to do, then it's better for me to just get out of the trade. Taking a $30, $50 loss is better than tying up the capital for three weeks, then rolling the trade, which would add another 50% more risk. To me, it just doesn't make sense to put all that effort over there.

Jane: So do you remember your biggest loss in your trading days and what that was?

Sarah: Yes, it was in futures. And honestly, that was me being too cocky and thinking... I was just getting too ahead of myself. At that time I had an amount that I was trying to make every day in futures. I think that I was starting to get really good at it and it was about time that the market kind of schooled me. I was just getting into trades because I felt like I needed to get into trades. Like, "Oh my gosh. I haven't hit my quota of trading five trades today," or whatever it is I was aiming for... I don't remember the number. But I know that I was pushing the envelope too much and I was just trying to focus on a target as opposed to looking for a good trade. And I got in the trade and it went wrong. And I was thinking I was so great, that this couldn't possibly happen, and I let that trade run too long. But you know what? I think every trader has that story, where they lost too much money on a trade...Even if I told other people, "Don't do this," it's almost like they have to have that experience for themselves to kind of figure that out. They'll be like, "Oh, yeah. I shouldn't have done that." So yeah, I had a bad futures trade that I would love to take back if I could.

Jane: Sometimes it's like that with little kids. Sometimes you just have to let them fall and stumble and hurt themselves because they just don't understand until they have experienced it. So they have to have that experience for themselves to learn; as much as you want to protect them 110%, sometimes people really need to feel that for themselves.

Sarah: Yes. And obviously, I want them to feel it so that they can still be around. To me, that's the saddest thing, when I get people who say, "Oh, I blew up my account." I haven't had that experience, and to me, that's devastating because that means you can't get up the next day and try again. So yes, I want everyone to have a loss, but I want you to still be able to learn from it and go apply to do something else the next day, to make it better.

Jane: And on the flip side, do you remember your largest win or gain that you had with a trade?

Sarah: No, actually. I don't. That's a great question. I don't know why I don't remember that. That may be more because my approach to trading is all about consistency. I don't ever try to get a million dollar trade; what I try to do is to be consistent. If I can have eight trades on that week and I have eight winners and I've made at least $30 a contract per win, then, as a minimum, that's really happy. So to me, it's just about hitting those targets, and I'm incredibly proud that I can do that time and time again. A couple weeks ago, I had a huge winner on Apple...

Jane: Very nice.

Sarah: Okay. Well, one thing I learned from speaking, because I do a lot of talks and trading for different brokers, and especially in the US, is that, as a Canadian, I had to learn to boast a bit or to realize... And maybe this is a female thing, to realize that you are good enough to be there, to stand proud and say, "Yes, I can do this really well." And that was something that was really hard for me to overcome. So even telling you, "Oh, yeah. No, I do really well," it still feels really awkward for me.

Jane: I was asked to talk to women about empowerment out in California and I said to myself, "This is surreal. I'm a mom here trading from my basement office." And it's weird that people see me as someone who's really influencing them when I'm just trying to share my experience and encourage others. But it's so much more than what other people do or what other people are comfortable with, and it's true: we do have a talent for it. So why not share it and help encourage instead of having people feel like they can't do it and being fearful about it? One of the biggest things, I think, is the fear mindset that people have in even stepping forward to try.

Sarah: Absolutely. So yeah, I guess I've got the answer. I guess I have lots of successes and I hit my goals, and, as I said, my goal was to grow the account by 5% a week.

Jane: Which is great; that's wonderful. Now, when you first got into trading, how would you say you handled the emotions? Because obviously you weren't necessarily consistent in the beginning.

Sarah: Oh, yeah. Where I am now is nowhere near where I was then. It's very, very different and it changes as you grow. So now, when I'm trading, I think I'm at that level of automaticity. So just like when you're driving a car, you don't really think about all the steps; you can kind of naturally do it now and you can get from point A to point B. This is different from back when you were learning standard and you were still stalling the car. Obviously it's the same thing with trading.

Jane: How did you handle your emotions with trading in the beginning?

Sarah: Oh, right. Emotions. That was a really tough thing to do, and that's probably the biggest hurdle. Anybody can learn a trade setup, but understanding how to manage your emotions is key. A big part of it for me was, first off, playing around with contract size. I quickly realized that if I kept my contract size small, I didn't get emotional, I didn't care as much. I didn't make a lot of decisions based on feelings; I made decisions based on evidence. And I tested it out a little bit, and that's what I always recommend for other people. You need to know your number. You need to know the number of contracts that you can get in, just under it, that you don't have what's called an amygdala hijack, where your brain, your emotional response is taking over with trading; that you are still able to make rational decisions. And the best way, like you're saying too, is to test it out in a paper account. Try trading with four contracts; try trading with five contracts. Until a trade doesn't work, that's the only time you're really going to figure out, "What does that feel like and how do I respond to it?" It's important to know what your number was, and I played around with that, and that was from a trading journal; just writing down how I felt as I placed different trades.

Then I decided that for one month at a time, I was going test the contract size. So for one month, I would just trade four contracts. The next month I would trade five contracts. And then I figured out where that level was for me that, "Okay, if I get up to 10, I don't like that feeling. But if I can stay under it at eight, I'm perfectly comfortable." I'd encourage other people to kind of do that process so they know what their number is. That's really important. And then the other piece... And again, this is where, I was saying, the books *Mindset* by Carol S. Dweck Potter and *Drive* by Daniel H. Pink are really important. Those aren't really trading books because it is about understanding how to break down trading in a way that is about gathering evidence. And the more I could make a good case for why I should place a trade, the less emotions I would make in my decision of trading. This also has to do with the fact that I have a Master's of Education in adult learning theory, so I applied a lot of the brain stuff that I had learned about how adults learn best to trading. That's really where this evidence piece came about. So I put it in my book too.

It's a three-column chart and it's called "I Do, I Don't, I Don't Know". And I did this over and over again, especially when I first started. I would just put it on either a sticky note or I used to have a kids' primary or elementary classroom school agenda book - one that has enough space for Monday, Tuesday, Wednesday, Thursday, Friday, for you to write in. I would put it there. So, on a three-column chart I would write down the evidence I have for the trade, what I don't have for the trade, and then what am I'm not really sure about. By coming back to that three-column chart all the time,

I found that it really helped me hone in on whether I was making the decision from an emotional state or whether it was actual evidence. And it's such a simple thing, but I found that to be very, very helpful. I would encourage other people to come up with some system where they're gathering evidence and then use that to make your decision. The moment you start saying, "I wish... I could have... " that's kind of like, "Oh, man."

Jane: The hope strategy.

Sarah: All that stuff, you have to recognize for sure is an emotional response. You need to pull it back to the evidence that you originally gathered. And physically writing that down can help with the rational process.

Jane: As far as your options, do you look at level two at all when you're trading your options, or are you just looking at the chart and the volume?

Sarah: I think the more information in an options chain that you can get, the better. What I do is kind of combine technical analysis and charting. I like to look at different time frames, and then I layer that with all the information in the options chain. In this way I am understanding things like how the bid and ask are moving and what the last trade was. I like to use Greeks in there as well, so paying attention to delta and theta is very helpful; open interest is also helpful. There's a story to be told in the options chain, this is what I always say. You've got to make sure you spend some time reading that story because the market makers are pricing in where they think the price is going, and you want to use that to help you trade. So the more information you have there, I think the better.

Jane: Now, with the market makers, do you typically tend to trade more New York Stock Exchange stocks or NASDAQ? Personally, I find there's a lot of market maker manipulation with NASDAQ equities.

Sarah: Oh, I can't say that I have noticed that. I would trade both. To me, it just depends on how well something's set up. I haven't seen a relationship there that would make me choose one or the other; it's just about if you've got the right evidence there from the beginning. It's never really mattered for me. And then it's also the same with options on futures, which is a newer product, and I guess weeklies are a newer product relative to monthlies. It all just depends on what trade is setting up well.

Jane: Who do you use for brokers and what platforms do you use for information? I know you're in Canada, so it's not going to be the same as many of the US brokers, but who are you using to trade the US options?

Sarah: The only disadvantage to Canadians, is we, I think, are the most regulated country for trading in the world. It seems like we have so many rules to jump through, and so we don't have the choices that other people do in the rest of the world. So, at this point I use Interactive Brokers because they're the cheapest. If I was in the States, you have so many more choices because you can get involved in Trade Station or thinkorswim. There are just so many platforms out there. We just don't have the choice in Canada, so that's why I trade Interactive Brokers.

Jane: Well, that's it. To me, I think that in Canada, you really have Quest Trade, Interactive Brokers, and I'm not even sure if thinkorswim or TD has a platform as well. So it is very much limited for who Canadians can trade with.

Sarah: Yeah, I would choose another one if I could, but I can't. In my book, I did a section on how finding a broker is kind of like going to a farmers' market: you need to sample each one and figure out which one you like because they all have different advantages and disadvantages.

Jane: And as far as being a female in the trading world, do you think that there were any hurdles for you coming into the trading world, or any hurdles today?

Sarah: Yeah, I actually think there are a lot of hurdles for women. There aren't a lot of women out there trading and I think that there should be more. One, because especially if you have a young family, it's a great way to still be involved with your kids and be able to trade. And just like we've talked about earlier, there aren't really a lot of people out there who are role models in this industry. It still remains a male-dominated place to be. So, I think the more of us who come out and talk, the better, so that we can level that playing field. And I just think, even with women, I want women to feel empowered to try it, but I want everybody to feel empowered to try it. This is not something that people need to be scared of. As long as it's learned like a skill, then anybody can do it. And I would love for more women to get involved in this and to feel that they can do it.

Jane: And as far as any rules that you use on a day-to-day basis, what would you recommend? Do you have any mental rules or rules that you have posted? I know you kept coming back to your chart in the beginning.

Sarah: I should be sponsored by Post-it notes because I find I keep Post-it notes beside my computer all the time. And especially when I was starting out. I had trading rules, and so I would write on a Post-it note my trading rules: "I'm looking for trend, five minutes timing, and ATR (average true range) etc." And if I get these things, I trade, and then I post that up on my wall on a Post-it note. When I was learning the concepts as well, I found it helpful to write down the definitions on Post-it notes. When I was learning, "What is call, what is a put? What does all that mean?" And that was a long time ago, but again, I would do a Post-it note for each one of those concepts and I'd have these up on my wall. So that wall, at the time, was just full of different points of information. But it was very helpful. Like a terminology wall, a word wall.

Jane: Well that's it. It's like some people have vision boards that they put up. And it can be the same sort of thing for trading that you have something out there where it's right in front of your face to remind you on a day-to-day basis.

Sarah: I think I am naturally a person who tries to figure something out and become better at it. So I just kind of did that internally.

Jane: Got it, and you have two kids. So how do you really balance your trading? Are your kids at daycare at all, or are they both at home now?

Sarah: They've never been in daycare. They're both with me. My three-year-old just started preschool, but they're around me a lot. I have someone who will come in and help me in the house. As we speak now doing this interview, I'm sitting on the floor, and my youngest is right beside me, and we're playing with chewy toys. I think you can trade with babies, and I'm so proud of that, that they are with me. I'm glad that they're a part of it, but it's not always easy. When my eldest was a baby and in the banging stage she traded for me unintentionally by banging on the keyboard. That wasn't so great. So I have those experiences too. It doesn't always work out brilliantly. I'm grateful for the times that I have a baby wrapped in my Ergobaby carrier and sleeping or nursing while I trade. My toddler will often play what she calls trading. She'll sit behind me while I'm trading, and she has her little setup. She has a keyboard herself, and a little journal, and she writes on Post-its. We're a little team, a trading team.

Jane: Very cute. And as far as traveling, you said that you tend to spend about six months of the year in California. Do you travel a lot with your trading?

Sarah: Yes. When I'm in California, I'm only there about three months, but yeah, I will trade from the beach or the porch. California's perfect because the Pacific Time, the time zone, helps really well for trading. You can just get up in the morning and then you're done by 1 pm PST. I've traded on an airplane. Every trading mom needs an Ergobaby carrier in my opinion; I can't live without it. The baby is in the carrier, and I'll be walking around and trading.

Jane: Well it's also comforting for her too, to be close to Mom.

Sarah: Yeah. And I want my girls to grow up in this world where they feel like they can try anything, and they don't need to be afraid because they are women. Women who are risk takers are great role models. Even if things don't work out exactly how we planned, showing girls that women can take risks is important. Women can help other women by being role models and pursuing whatever passions we all desire. I just want them to feel like they can do it too. So I like to have them included. And, oh, here's another funny thing too. My eldest doesn't know what Chipotle is, but she knows what CMG is. So CMG is the stock symbol, but she thinks that's the name of the restaurant. And if you ask, "Are we going to go to CMG to eat?", she knows what that means.

Jane: Very cute. How long would you say, in your trading journey, it took you to feel successful?

Sarah: I think it takes a full year to be really good at it because I also think you need to be involved in the market for a long time. I think it takes about a year because it's one thing to work out a strategy for a month, but you need to see the markets shift. The summer market is a slower market; it's different than what January will be. I think you need a full year of trying out trade setups.

Jane: Okay. And how long was it until you felt successful enough so that you could go into it as your career?

Sarah: It took me a lot longer. For a long time, I never thought I was good enough to actually share what I was doing. It took me a long time before I realized, "I actually know a lot more than a lot of other people do." And I always thought everyone else knew more than me. It took a

117

long time to garner that self-confidence to come out and say, "You know what? I am going to trade in the public and I'm okay." Because every time I trade, I'm always trading live and with real money; I think that's really important. When I first started my first talk, I was like, "Wow. I know a lot more than other people do." And I never thought I did.

Jane: Yes, it all adds up cumulatively, and before you know it, you're talking and people are curious: "Where did you learn all this knowledge and how do you know all this stuff?"

Sarah: Yeah.

Jane: I agree.

Sarah: And there's a real difference from textbook knowledge. You can have textbook knowledge, but you need trading knowledge that comes from actually having an account and being in the market every day.

Jane: You assimilate it from going to school, university, or college, and then you go into your internship, and you actually get the hands-on experience, which is invaluable compared to what you can learn from a book. You have to have that hands-on experience.

Thank you, Sarah, for your time and contribution to the book

Justine Pollard

Australia

Twitter: @justinepollard
Website: smarttrading.com.au
YouTube: smarttradingjp
Book: *Smart Trading Plans*

I first found Justine by Googling female traders. I then explored her site and was intrigued with her success with trading and her trading systems. It amazes me that women around the world have found success in trading. It is not only a non-discriminatory career but one that can be done anywhere in the world. Justine's experiences while trading through the fall of the World Trade Towers brings new light to proper exit strategies.

Jane: How did trading become your career?

Justine: I came to trading from my grandfather. My husband and I met in high school. We had both been working part-time. I've been working part-time since I was 11. I used to work at the local news agency, or do babysitting jobs. In Australia, you can't get your real part-time job until you're 14 years and nine months. At 14 years and nine

119

months, I got my job at Donut Dan making donuts. I was always right into earning money. My parents didn't have a lot of money. If I wanted something, I had to save up for it.

I had to save up for my car. I had to basically get everything for myself. I'm glad that I had to do those things. It made me a better money manager. I saved up a good bank account when I left high school and I wasn't quite ready to buy a car yet, either. My grandfather said, "You should put some money into shares." And I said, "Well, what would you suggest?" He named four blue chip shares that he owned in his portfolio that were high dividend yield shares. My husband (who was my boyfriend at that time) did the same after talking to his grandfather and he agreed on the same shares. Both of our grandfathers owned shares and used fundamental analysis to build up a portfolio of high yield dividend shares. They lived off the dividends they received.

You could buy anything in the 1990s and you would make money. It was a phenomenal bull market until about '97. We entered the market at the beginning of '92. We had finished high school in '91. We got the share trading account set up during the holidays after school finished, and then we bought into those shares in the New Year. It was a process back then to open a share account, not like these days where you can open an account on the same day.

We bought into these four shares. We held them until 1996, and that's when we sold them to buy our first investment property. We had that great experience because those shares all went up and we doubled our money on a few of them. We were still working, so we still had cash, and in selling those shares we had a nice deposit for our first place. We bought our first place, which we rented out. We had no money after that. We couldn't leverage off anything yet until we had equity growth in our property and had paid some of the mortgage down.

It was '99 when I got back into the market. I continued reading. I had previously been motivated by *Rich Dad, Poor Dad* by Robert Kiyosaki and Sharon Lechter. My whole goal was just for that financial freedom. Making my money work hard for me is what I really learned from that book. Yes, I can work hard for my money, but I need that money to then work hard for me as well. That's the big take out. I wanted to invest that money and keep it growing. I kept learning and I went to a lot of property investment seminars. In '99, there was a series of seminars that also included information on trading. I went to the first intro night and I really liked it.

My husband and I then went to the big weekend event. The best thing the instructordid was basically break us all up into groups. Everybody at that time was living in city northern beaches. He said everybody who lives in city northern beaches, go to that corner. Sydney West, go over there, and so on. I met a group of about 20 people. We all really hit it off. We had monthly meetings. We then went to the next seminar that this guy held. He doesn't run seminars or do any of this anymore. It was run on Hamilton Island and we went as a group. We called ourselves the Beach Billionaires. We actually created a uniform and went to the event as the Beach Billionaires and learned even more strategies on property investing and options trading.

It was pretty much after that event that my husband and I decided, "Well, I wonder if we could make a living out of this." We were in a comfortable position. We had paid most of the mortgage down from renting the property before we moved into it. Without kids we could easily live off my husband's income. So we made the decision for me to leave my full-time job and learn to trade and make a go of these so called strategies. At the end of 2000, I gave notice and started trading full-time in 2001. I had been trading on the side as a hobby prior to this. We had set ourselves up with a self-managed superfund and I was trading the strategies through this to start with.

I was trying to do some options trading while I was working. Really short term trading isn't quite a good strategy while you're working. I did some sort of options trading against the share portfolio and a few other things. I really wanted to do more strategies full-time. We made that decision and I did. I started trading full-time. From that trading group, we met up regularly. We shared ideas. We used to get other traders to come and speak to our group and my trading evolved as I learned more. There were four of us from the group who did not work and we could meet more regularly to discuss trading ideas.

We took different courses together and bought courses as a group. It really honed and played with our skills. Fiona, who I became very good friends with, was a stay-at-home mom. She was part of this group. She was also a programmer and was able to write codes and we could play around with things. None of us could make the strategies work that we'd learned from the original seminars where we had met. We all gave it a go. They're great strategies if it's a sideways market as they involve writing calls against your share portfolio. When the market is moving higher, your shares keep getting exercised each month and you have to keep buying the share back. It would have been better to have held the shares and just let them rise.

I just kept getting exercised for small amounts of money and having to enter it in at a higher price again and do the prices again. We all ended up calling it quits on the strategies that we'd learned from his seminar. The property stuff we had learned was great, but the share trading and options did not work. The problem with the share trading strategies is that there were no exits taught. We all tried to give it a go. None of us could make it work. We had that passion to make it work. We kept going. That's pretty much the journey that got me to the full-time trading. Then the big kick up the backside in September 11. This is what I needed to get back on track because I would've eventually gotten the big kick up the backside doing high risk strategies like that. Just was not worth it in the end.

Jane: If you don't mind, Justine, can you tell me about that experience?

Justine: During that first year of trading (which was 2001) as a full-time trader, that's when the World Trade Center crash happened. I started off doing different option strategies that I had learned over time. I was mostly attracted to the fast-paced action of options and thinking that the more I traded and the shorter-term I traded, the more money I would make. Then I learned about naked writing of options. You can make money without needing any capital. I thought, "This is fantastic." I had some shares and I could use these shares as collateral for the margin required. It just seemed too easy. I didn't need any money. I could write these options.

I started writing more and more options every month, and then I started writing put options as the market was going up and writing put options is a great strategy when the market is rising. Then the World Trade Center crash happened. I had a whole lot of written puts open in the market just before The World Trade Center crash occurred. I had come back from holidays. On Monday, I opened up the market in Australia and it was running really well on the upside. It looked great to have some naked puts running because it was going up. I had a whole series of naked puts in place.

Then, it was the Wednesday morning in Australia after the World Trade attacks had occurred overnight. I had naked puts open. The scariest part of that day was I knew I had to get out because my stops were hit, and I was always vigilant on that. It was the fact that I couldn't get out. The options market makers just wouldn't make a market to start with because the volatility of the banks was so extreme. Then when they started making a market, my broker would put the trade in, and they moved the spread so wide that I couldn't get the trade executed. It was like a bunch of cowboys trying to get my trades away.

My broker had to keep working and working it. We finally got them closed at the end of the trade day. We had another two or three days of the market dropping as well; it would've gotten worse before we finally got the rebound the following week. I basically lost all my profits that I had made that whole year plus some of my capital. I was in a losing situation. My trading account was down by 10 percent. I was in a loss after all that trading over the year. I just felt like everything I'd done for the whole year was a waste of time. All the profits were gone and now I'd taken a loss. I had nothing left to show for my trading.

That's when I realized, do I want to do this? Do I want to keep doing this? This just did not seem worth it. For three weeks, I probably went inside myself and just really assessed whether this was something I wanted to keep doing. I also then had a good look at my self-managed super fund that was holding long term trades. They had all done very well with very little work. It was a bit of an eye opener for me to realize that those hours I'd spent in front of the screen trading options and taking on board too high risk strategies just were not worth it. The strategies I was doing, like writing naked options, I wouldn't even dream of doing now.

When things are working and going very well, you can take on board more risk and that is what I had been doing. I believe if the World Trade Center crash hadn't happened, I still eventually would've got that big kick up the backside because I was doing very high risk strategies and wasn't managing any sort of total open market at that time. It was going to happen sooner or later. It was better that it happened sooner rather than later, that I didn't lose even more.

I'm actually grateful for that experience now. I wasn't at the time. It was like I was in a big black hole. I was an emotional mess for at least a week. Then, I got a bit better and got the courage to reassess things. It took me three weeks to find the courage to consider that I still wanted to do this, but something had to change.

Jane: After your experience with the fall of the Towers and everything, then you developed your trading strategy. Correct? You started your trading strategy in 2002?

Justine: I had enrolled in a trading course. Since it was already booked, I decided that I would still do the trading course. After doing that trading course, the person hosting the event said that's the first time he'd experienced a terrorist attack. I realized that it was something completely out of my control. The market is completely out of your control when you don't know what's going to happen to any trade at any time.

It takes some time to become comfortable with that. The only way to become comfortable is to have money management and exit rules. I had money management rules, but I wasn't managing a total portfolio heat and I was overtrading. I went back to Van Tharp's work and bought a couple more of his courses and his money management report. I knew that if I was going to continue to trade, things had to change. CFDs became available in 2002 in Australia. I decided to build up a strategy with CFD's. I bought one course of the key strategies. I then bought one about portfolio heat on the total market to help me manage my total market open risk. I didn't want to experience another World Center crash, but if it were to happen again, I couldn't stop myself from experiencing it.

Now, I always manage a five percent portfolio heat across my trades. If I was first starting out, I could open up five trades risking one percent of my capital. That wouldn't mean I was only buying one percent of the trade size. That's the difference between my stop loss and my entry price divided by one percent of my capital. That's how many shares I could buy. If it hits my stop loss, then I would lose one percent of my capital. I know that on any one trade, I won't lose more. Occasionally, yes, I get slippage. I can lose more, but it's not usually that much more.

I always manage my portfolio to make sure that I don't lose any more than five percent of my capital in one go. If I was starting a new portfolio, I'd go out and open my five trades. I couldn't open another trade until some of those stop losses started moving my way and created another one percent of available risk and my portfolio heat drops from five percent down to four percent. Then I could open up another trade risking one percent. I'm always managing my worse case draw down.

When the market's running really well, my portfolio heat is constantly going down because my stop losses are moving. I know that I'm in the zone of trading. I'm riding a good wave; I can keep on opening up positions. Once I'm on a winning trade and there are profits there, I can use some of those profits and pyramid and buy more. That does affect my portfolio heat because I'm actually using profits within a trade to buy more. It's more about managing how many new trades I can have open at once.

The biggest risk on any one trade is getting your stop loss from the initial stop to break even. Once I'm at break even, I'm not risking anything; it doesn't affect my portfolio hit anymore. The biggest risk is in those initial stages when you first buy the shares. You get to have some trades, you buy, and that was the last high made. If it's a long trade, it'll be the last low. If it's a short trade, then you just get stopped out. There's nothing you can do about it. I've kept that to one percent of my capital. Then the goal is to get bigger trades. This is for medium to long term trades. You need bigger wins out there.

Day trading is a completely different type of strategy that you've used, but you probably don't overexpose yourself. You probably have a selection of shares that you like to watch and that's all you're going to trade for the day. You'll only have so many positions open at once, then they're all closed at the end of the day. See, I carry my trades over and we'll have them open overnight. My average hold time with my daily swing trading varies between 25 to 30 days.

I can have a winning trade open for 90 days. I can have a losing trade open for 10 days; you know what I mean? It averages out to be about 25 to 30 days. I find that it's about 30 days in good trading markets at the moment because the market's consolidating; it's dropped down to about 25 days. With my longer term system, I'm happy to hold things for years if they're going to keep going my way. That's where it's important. I'm keeping trades open. You're not keeping any trades open. You might run things slightly differently, but you don't need to be running so many trades a day at any one time.

Jane: Correct. In your trading systems, how many trades do you typically have open at one time? Is it five, 10, or is it just up to the maximum that your account will allow you to invest at a certain point at time?

Justine: Yeah, it's basically dependent on my portfolio heat At a certain point of time it's the portfolio hitting my capital that determines how many I can have open. Right now, I've just opened up my spreadsheet over 1, 2, 3, 4, 5, 6, 7, 8, 9, 10, 11, 12, 13, 14... I've got 14 trades running. Three of them are short trades right now that are fully invested with the daily swing trading system. I can't do any more at the moment until I get stopped out or exit a trade based on certain things happening. I'm in that nice position where I'm fully invested right now. In this sideways market it hasn't been like that for quite a while. That's how many I got with the daily swing trading system.

The long term weekly system right now has five trades open. I've been a bit slower building into it because the market's consolidating. I don't know if we're going to get into that healthy market and if we're going to get the breakout. I'm happy to keep my five trades open and let them unfold and build onto them. I'd like to hold some money back to pyramid with those ones. Those five trades are going really well.

I've had some that I've exited out of, but I've built up some nice trades. You know what I mean? I'll be in and out of some until I get those five, or up to seven or eight would probably be at complete maximum. Then I just leave them running. There's nothing more I can do with them except for pyramid as I go my way.

Jane: Very nice. Now, you said in your day trading one or your shorter term one, you have long and short. Do you typically tend to go long or short? What's your preference?

Justine: That completely depends on what the trading system's bringing out for me. I don't have a preference. I'm going with the strongest part of the market at any point in time. I'm happy to do either. At the moment, there are three in the market, mostly being long, but I have two really good short signals that just lined up great. The market's also sitting at quite a resistance point right now. I've felt quite comfortable to have those short trades there. There will be times when I'm net long; there will be times when I'm net short. For probably the last two years, I've mostly had a mix in there.

There will be periods where the market will be running. I'll be mostly long. Then, it starts turning, the stocks stop getting hit, and I just naturally end up having some short trades open. Then, we'll be consolidating the consolidation phase; it's just what's happening. There's no preference to me. I'm just taking the strongest signal on the day. If it's a short trade, it's a short trade. If it's a long trade, it's a long trade.

Jane: I hear you.

Justine: I'll run the scan and the strength of the scan; I know where the strength is that day. If I run the scanner and only two come up on the short side or 10 or 15 come up on the long side, then I know the long side of the market was stronger that day and I'm more than likely going to take a long trade out of the market. That's where the strength is.

Jane: Great. I hear you talking about your scan. What is your typical trading day like?

Justine: In the morning, I always check what happened overnight in the US market. I just got an app on my phone. I can just click on that. I can see the S&P 500, Dow Jones, and I also have gold and oil in there. In Australia, we're predominantly a resource country. We have a lot of mining stocks on the stock market. When gold is running, I'll be long gold. If gold's full, then I'll be short. Not gold in general. I have traded gold; I actually prefer to trade the shares. I find that I get higher profit potential out of the shares than the gold itself. They move with the gold, but they can sometimes move better than gold.

I will always know before a market opens how to feel for what's happened out there unless it's been a huge drop overnight in the US market. Then the expectations are that we're going to open down for the day. Not to say we won't recover by the end of the day; we may recover. If I'm trading shares like BHP, ResMed, those types of shares that trade on the overseas markets, then I've got an expectation of how that will open. Generally, I don't look at the market. I only just opened up my trading screen now, so I can tell you how many trades I have open.

Generally, I'm not looking at the market until after 3 pm. The Aussie market closes at 4 pm. Depending on what my afternoon's like, if the kids don't have any activities or they don't have anything on until after 4 o'clock, I'll start to have everything open just before 3 o'clock. If I'm picking them up from school, this is what I used to do. Most of the time my husband picks up them up now, so I don't have to. I was just talking about when I was the only one at home. I would basically have my trading screen open and the charting software open.

As soon as we get home, I give the kids an afternoon tea. At 3:30, I just click the button. It downloads the data based on the 3 o'clock data. I can only download after 20 past the hour. Then I have the 3 o'clock data and I run my scanner on the 3 o'clock data. It doesn't matter if it is 3:40 or 3:45; I can do it all in 10 or 15 minutes.

I will then open up Metastock. I use Metastock. I have a quick scan through my open positions. I've checked my smart traders' spreadsheet and I know whether I can open a trade today based on my portfolio heat or my capital. I look at my open positions: is there anything, any action that needs to be taken, in relation to any of those positions? Also, I get a feel for whether I'll be moving any stop losses tonight. Then I run the scan. If I know I can open a trade, if there's something that I see that I like, I will place the trade.

I will look at all the charts that come up in all of those scans. I will narrow it down. Anything with immediate resistance for long trades or immediate support for short trades, I'll just cut. I'm left with a small number, maybe one, two, or three. Then, to look at those stocks and choose which one I'll open a position. As the trade that I choose from my position size and calculator and simply place the trade before the market closes on the platform, which I just do at market because the market's closing soon, I don't want to fiddle around with a small price fluctuation. I just want to get in there. I just get in with a stop loss set. That's it. The trading day is finished.

I'll already know whether any trades have gone my way, and whether I need to move any stop losses that night when I get the final data download from the final market close. I can move the stops based on the 6 o'clock data download. That's usually pretty accurate, but the final data download is available after 8 pm in case there were any errors from my data provider. The errors will be fixed up in that final download. I'll already know if I need to move any stops that night. I need to see the final closing price to know where the stops are going to be sitting.

Jane: From your scans, when you're looking at the charts, are there certain indicators that you're looking for to help you decide if you really want to go into it, besides the support and resistance?

Justine: Yes. You cant code everything in a scan. There's not one magic number or anything out there. There's no holy grail. So I've got on my chart the moving average. I look at everything in the candlestick format with the 30 period moving average. I have the volume with the 30 period moving average over the volume. I have the average true range indicator, which is purely for position sizing. I have the MACD-histogram.

The other thing I'll look at if I've got more than one share to choose from is the MACD-histogram. I call it my decision-making tool. If one share has divergence and the other one doesn't, then I'll pick the one that doesn't. Basically, breaking out or retracing is the reason that comes up in the scan. It's making a new high or it's having a retracement.

Jane: You developed these systems in order to trade different stages in the market.

Justine: Market stages. I still add things to watch these. Sometimes I might see something and it might not be quite right. Or maybe the move today had a beautiful breakout, but it was too big a move. I would then put on a watch for a pull back. The system is giving me the signal, but I might wait and hold back on the entry if it's too big a swing. I call it a swing trading system. If it's had too big a swing already, I'm not going to enter into it. The swing has already happened. I want to get into the earlier part of the swing. I might put it on the watch list, but if it pulls back and bounces, then I'll get into the retracement of the swing.

Jane: What are those four stages of the market again?

Justine: It's following the Stan Weinstein book called *How to Profit in Bull and Bear Markets*. You've got the stage one base; you've got the stage two up trend, which is the healthy part. That's the one that my long term system wants to capitalize on. You've got the stage three top; that's where my long term system will start to get out of the positions and exit. You've got the stage four downtrend. That's when my long term system will not be trading, but I will be actively short selling my daily swing trading system. After stage four downtrend the market will usually bottom out again and will start to move back into a stage one base.

That stage one base may be very quick, or it could go sideways for a period of a year before it starts going up and becoming healthy again. I basically go long in my daily system in stage two uptrends and short in stage four downtrends. I'll find I'll be both long and short when the market is in that basing stage and that stage three top stage. During these stages I will do extra things like employ an aggressive exit strategy as the market is mostly in consolidation phase. That's from me looking at the index charts and the number of new shares making new weekly highs to lows and where the strength is.

If I'm seeing that equilibrium happening, then I know we're in that consolidation phase and I know that it's important to use my aggressive exit strategy. When we're in a bull market, you feel it; you're mostly long in the market. You're getting beautiful signals. Everything's moving. My portfolio heat keeps going down. I'm becoming fully invested in the market during that time. When the market hits the sideways stage; you start to feel the frustration of the market. The big winners just aren't out there. The only way I can capitalize on them is by employing the aggressive exit strategy, which I mentioned. I introduced this aggressive exit strategy in 2010 after hitting a cluster of losses. It had been quite a long time since I'd had that happen. That's when I knew the market had changed.

Jane: How did having your daughter in 2005 affect your trading?

Justine: For me, I already had my trading systems set up. I was at that stage where it wasn't taking up much of my time. I was in a good position for doing that. I actually still had positions open even when I was giving birth. You don't know when you're going to go into labor. Both my kids were overdue. I could still keep trading. I still had positions open. Nowadays, you've got everything on your phone. I can log into the app with my broker and see where my positions stand, and I can actually exit a trade off my phone. It's just so much easier. You've got everything in your hands now with your phone.

I can't run my market scans on my phone. I need to be in front of the computer to do that. I can check my positions. When I go on holidays, I stop opening up positions, depending on where I'm going and for how long I'm going. If I'm going overseas, I completely shut down my daily swing trading systems and just keep my weekly long term systems open being that it is a longer term system. It doesn't matter if I don't move any stop losses for a couple of weeks, but I will shut down my daily swing trading systems. If I'm going on holidays, I need to take a break from the markets as well.

If I'm just traveling within Australia, I will still keep some of my swing trades open. I might stop opening up some fresh new trades because the biggest risk on any trade is when you first open them. We went away during a school holiday in April. Just recently we went away for a week. We were only in Australia, so I kept my trades open. I even opened up a trade. There was one moment when we were back at the hotel room. It was about 2:30. I ran my scanner, and there was this short trade that was just so beautiful. I was like, "Ah." I just got into it. I just opened that. That was the only trade I opened while I was away. I still have it open now. It's still doing well.

It had its big fall, and then it consolidated a bit. Once my trading stop is in profit, the time stop doesn't matter anymore. I'm happy to stick with it then. That one is still open and running. I can have that flexibility. Most of the time, 3:30 is my favorite trading time. When I'm away, I might run a scanner in the evening and look at some trades. I might check my open positions and think tomorrow I should do a check up, better keep an eye on that position tomorrow. Now that the market is going good, I don't have to do anything; I don't worry about anything.

I have that flexibility of running the scan early in the day. I don't really like running it any earlier than the 2:30 scan. That would be 2 o'clock data because that market closes at 4. That would be the earliest that I would actually trade. I do like the 3 o'clock, or otherwise I will wait. I have flexibility where I can change it to suit if the kids have something one afternoon, if we get caught up at the school, or if they'd like to bring friends home. Things happen. If one of them has hurt themselves outside, you just have to drop everything and not trade.

If I can't trade, it's not a big deal. My stop losses are set with my broker. I've got my trading set up where it's not a big deal. When my daughter was a baby, I was still trading. If I couldn't trade at 3:30, it didn't matter. I had my stops in place. It's about not being too hard on yourself in your life when other things are going on. I like the flexibility of trading because you can turn it on and off if you need to. I always got my weekly long term system running. There are times when that might be running while the other one's turned off, or vice versa because we're in a bear market.

One thing that I did find when I had my daughter was to just not be too hard on myself. If I didn't get to trade this week because I was sleep-deprived and my head space wasn't there, it doesn't matter. Just don't be too hard on yourself. The idea is that I wanted to be the super mom who could do everything. I was trying to do this, but I wasn't coping as a mom. Something had to give.

My daughter had colic; she had allergies. She would scream from 5 to 7 o'clock for no reason. I didn't know what it was; it was colic and the allergies building up at the end of the day. I was breastfeeding her while eating all the foods that she was allergic to. I didn't know that at the time. I learned all that six months down the track. When I stopped feeding her those foods, it made a difference. I had to be a bit easier on myself and tone things back a bit. Then, when things got well, I could tone things up. Sometimes you got to tone things back because the market just isn't suitable to be trading at that particular time.

There are other reasons why you might tone things back if things just aren't going well in the market. That's what I did in 2010; I cut back because I hit that cluster of losses. Something was not working. I still liked being in the market, so I just cut things back. Then I just started looking at what was going on and brought that aggressive exit strategy. I do talk about the new trading plan; you need to have psychological exits as well.

If you're moving to a new house, if someone in the family passed away, or if something's happening in your relationship, you'll take it out in the market. I've got one client who was going through a divorce and he upped his trading because he believed that the market owed him with everything else that was going on. He just made everything worse. He was taking it out on the market in the end. From what we were talking about before, women would probably emotionally go, "I just can't do this right now." Take that step back from it all. There are times when you need to know yourself as a trader too, and when you're not performing at that higher level, cut your trading back.

For a new person starting out, give yourself some time to learn and hone that skill. It's like starting a brand new job. You've got no idea what you're doing. You need to basically learn, and the biggest thing I can recommend for anybody before they start is to write a trading plan first. You need to have a strategy. You can just buy hot tips and things, but what's the strategy to get out? There is none. You need to have that whole strategy, no matter what your reasoning is while you're entering or what your reason is for getting out. That's the most important thing.

You can go out there and buy a whole lot of shares and put them in a portfolio. You only need one or two of them that disappear off the stock market. In Australia, we've had many shares disappear off the stock market. We've just had Dick Smith recently disappear off the stock market. If you were holding on to them in the hope that they would get better, you pretty much wiped out all your profits for the year with all your good trades as well.

It's very important to have that exit strategy, but take the time to learn. Start off with a small trading account, or even a demo account, or paper trading if you have to while you're learning and practicing those skills. When you're ready, put your real money in the market. You'll learn a whole lot more once your real money goes into market. That's when the real experience starts. That's when your apprenticeship starts.

Jane: Once you pay your dues and tuition fee to the market.

Justine: Yeah. I found I probably had more time when my kids were younger to trade because daycare is a longer day than school. Once my kids started school, there are so many activities going on at the school where they want parents to be present. When I dropped them off at daycare, I didn't have to pick them up until pick-up time. I didn't have to go and watch their assemblies, their special events that they're doing, and Grandparents' Day. The athletics carnivals, the cross-country, the swimming carnival. I actually found out I had less time once my kids started school.

Jane: That's interesting, very interesting.

Justine: It's a shorter day, nine until three. I had an eight until five window when they were in daycare. While they are in daycare, make the most of that time because you have a lot more time on your hands to really learn. You have to think of it like starting a brand new job and learning a new skill and studying. You have to put the time into studying and honing that new skill. Work on yourself.

As women, we're really hard on ourselves. We beat ourselves up inside our heads a lot. You really have to learn with trading that ... To me, a losing trade isn't wrong. As long as I follow my trading rules and I got out my stop loss, that trade was still right. We make losing trades wrong. You have to be okay. It's all about keeping those losses minimal and those winning trades much bigger. That's what it's all about. If you can, start that trading system.

I believe once they go to high school - and my daughter will be in high school next year - you don't go to as much anymore. While they're in what we call primary school, which goes for us from kinder to year six, there are a lot of things that go on that I find I'm going down to the school for. My whole reason for wanting to trade the stock market was so that I could stay at home and so that I could go and do things with the kids and be at the school for things when they come up. I wanted to enjoy and not miss those opportunities because I was working a full-time job and couldn't go watch the athletics, or I couldn't go watch them on stage at the assembly when they were speaking.

The idea for me of wanting to be a mom and being that trader was I could be there for my kids and I could do all those things. I am: I'm there for them. They just know I'm not there for them between 3:30 and 4 o'clock and that's when I trade.

Jane: That's your time; that's all right. Half an hour out of the day, you can have that for yourself.

Justine: Yeah. You can make trading as stressful as you want. In my early days of trading, I thought that the more I traded, the more money I would make. So I would also trade in the evenings. I was running trades on the US market and the Australian market. I started to find it was affecting my sleep. I was also doing commodities and indices trading, but then I would actually stay up watching the market for longer. If I woke up in the night, I would also want to check the market. It was like going and feeding a baby. You wake up and go, "Aah, I wonder what the market's doing?" You check your phone and it affects your sleep.

Whatever you do, find a trading style that suits your lifestyle. Try to not put too much pressure on yourself until you're in that good head space and you have that extra time to do those things. For me, I know my lifestyle right now is not suitable for...trading 24-hour markets. I like my sleep. I know that all my trading is finished at 4 o'clock, and I can't do anything. The most I can do is change stop losses. I can have the evening then with my family. It's finding out what suits you.

I've got another friend and his trading time, I think, is when the kids go to bed. He trades for two hours and that's his trading time. He's completely able to walk away from the market and go to sleep. Everybody's different with what suits them. Sometimes you have to go on a journey and you have to try different things to realize what's right for you and what's not right for you.

I didn't want trading to be another stress in my life. That's what I worked out, because I was making an extra stress in my life by trading too much and trading too many different things. You can trade 24 hours a day if you want to, except on the weekends. You can trade 24 hours a day.

Jane: Did you find any hurdles in going into trading as a woman?

Justine: There weren't many of us around. I did make a good friend, Fiona, as I mentioned, from this trading group. The two of us used to meet up with the two other gentlemen. She stopped trading for a while as she moved into property investing and became a mortgage broker. Now she's back to trading. She does more long term now. Just with the timing of kids in her life and starting a new business, she had to take a break from it and got right into the property side of things. We also do property investing. I've got a portfolio of properties in the US. I've got properties in a couple of states in the US. My strategy for property investing is positive cash flow. I don't want the properties to be costing me money to have.

I have other investments; I'm in a property development fund as well. There are a couple of other things that I do. Trading is the thing that I love. The US properties are something that we got set up for my husband to run and look after as well, that we can both do. He's not interested in the stock market. I always say he surfs the waves of the ocean and I surf the waves of the stock market. I find there's probably not as many of us.

From the people I teach, I find that the women are the ones who will take the time to learn and write the trading plan. The men are the ones who are just trading and doing it. The men tend to put the trading plan off until they get that huge big kick up the backside and realize that they should've done that a long time ago. They just want to be in the market. The fear of missing out is too strong. I will usually be teaching them while they're trading and making all the mistakes. They just have to be in the market.

They also say that it's younger men more so with their testosterone levels bringing on the aggressiveness in them. They just want to be in there. I've done a few interviews on why women make better traders than men. It's the testosterone that drives all the men to be doing these things without taking the time to learn, hone the skill, and write the trading plan.

Jane: I hear you.

Justine: Then some women can be a bit slow and have a lot of fears. It takes them a lot longer to get started and to make that first trade. There are plusses and minuses to both sides.

Jane: This might be a somewhat personal question, but have you had any issues with your success in your relationship with your husband? Do you think that sometimes the male ego makes them think, "I want to be the provider for the family." Then, you've turned out to be so successful, that's your role now.

Justine: No. Well, to start with, my husband was the provider, so I could learn to trade. It did take a couple of years before I saw the money coming in. The amount of money that I spent on educating myself, the amount of books, courses, and things I paid for ... I call it a uni degree basically. Trading is not a zero sum game. I've got my brokerage cost; I've got my charting software. I've got my data that I've got to pay for to get the charting software running, and to get the data for the charting software.

Because my husband's a surfer, in a way, I was always jealous. I always felt that he was a lot more easygoing than me. He got out in the ocean; he cleared his head. I'm probably the high strung one. Now he's actually taken a redundancy. He's now the stay-at-home dad. This has only happened in the last year. When I was talking about the stay-at-home mom, I was talking about when it was just me at home with the kids. Now, I'm actually the main provider.

The US properties have replaced his income. We've got that running for him. I've got my share trading running for me. That's how we do it. He's now running around with the kids and going to all the activities, and loving it. He had never been to an athletics carnival; he had never been able to go to the assemblies. He had never been able to do any of all these things I was doing. He is loving it. I'd never thought I'd see him cook. He's cooking now. He's taking it on board way better than I was expecting.

Jane: Great.

Justine: I don't know; not all men are the same. My husband was brought up with a single mother.. I think he's probably had a lot more females around him since a very young age where it was just him and his mom for a long time.

Jane: I'm certain it helps that you all were already together throughout it. He was supporting you going through it. He wanted to see you succeed for yourself and for the family, overall.

Justine: Yeah. He's seen me go through the bad times. He saw me through the World Trade Center crash and everything. It was me putting the pressure on myself at that time because I had come from quite a good job earning quite a bit of money. I was trying to make up for it in the market. He kept saying to me, "You know that I'm bringing the income in; your goal is just to learn, not put all this pressure on yourself." I did. I put way too much pressure on myself to try because I felt like I wasn't bringing any money. Previously, I had been. I felt like I put that pressure more on myself.

He didn't seem to have any resentment in any way. If anything, he's reaping the rewards now and quite enjoying it. Every now and then, he says, "Maybe I should try trading." I don't think we could cope if we were both trading at the time. I'd think that would be a bit competitive. He leaves that to me.

I leave different parts of our other investing to him. If anything, it's quite good. When my daughter came along, I remember him saying to me, "This is what you were like when you first started trading. Do you remember that first year of trading?" He said that is what I was like when my daughter was born. I just felt like I was out of control. That out of control feeling where you have this child that is so dependent on you and you couldn't make them sleep when they didn't want to sleep. You just had no control.

When you first start the market, you realize you have no control over the stock market. This lack of control actually brings up a lot of fears, such as after the World Trade Center crashed and I felt out of control. That was a huge one for me. I spent that whole year realizing that there is just completely no control over what the stock market could do. The only control I have is my money management. That's it. Yes, he's watched me go through different levels of journeys over time.

That's why we liken it to him surfing. He'll go out there and he'll have a good surf some days because the waves are good. It'll be crap other days. The stock market's like that too. It'll be fantastic, and you're enjoying the ride, and other times it's like you're so frustrated by it. You're wondering why you're even trading at this moment right now because the market's just horrible and you're going to take your losses. You're going to have periods of taking your losses.

I run a portfolio heat. Basically, I know my maximum draw down. If I have all of my stops get hit, then I know how much I will lose. That's when I actually say to myself, "What's happening in the market? Why have all my stops been hit? Is my system not working now?" Especially if that happens twice, where I have that draw down at five percent twice. That happened in 2010. We had a phenomenal bull market between 2003 and 2007. That was just fantastic. I was really building up my trading capital and I just kept reinvesting. I didn't take any money out; I just kept reinvesting everything to build up a good enough capital base so I could continue to reap the benefits of the returns.

Then, the GFC hit. I basically had all my stop losses in place. I was mostly short in my daily swing trading system because my swing trading system wasn't bringing up many strong long trades. I think I was net short with the swing trading system. My stop losses and my weekly systems started to get hit slowly between August, September, October, and the last trade went in January 2008. I remember that was a beautiful long term trade that I had pyramided. I got lots of dividends on it. Then the stock was hit and it was gone. I had that one for maybe two years.

I loved the GFC. I loved shorting. The fact that you can make money on falling shares - I just love that fact. I was really able to hone in and just short my daily swing trading system. Then 2009, mid-2009, the market really bottomed out. Then it started to kick up. We had a nice run from mid-2009 up until sometime in 2010. Then we consolidated and went sideways. That was very difficult market to trade. Trading markets are beautiful;

that's when you get the good returns. The consolidation periods can go on for years. From 2010 until pretty much the start of 2013, we were consolidating. I think most of the world markets were.

Then we took off again. The market started to become healthy again. But it did not last, as I then saw all my stops get hit and they continued to get hit. I was completely frustrated. What's going on here?

That's when I took a step back and had a look at the market and said, "Well, we've completely come off the highs. I can see the support and resistance building up." I felt what I was doing right then was not working. That's when I developed my aggressive exit strategy. I added on a channel trading strategy. If I wanted to continue trading through the sideways period, I needed to have a different strategy. When I had that cluster of losses hit, I toned things back. I had my risk levels in the market. I was trading smaller positions.

Then I was honing and introducing that aggressive strategy. I thought, I'm entering things. They were going okay for a little bit, and then my stop got hit. I was just frustrated. Small profits and losses. I just wasn't making anything. There simply weren't any big winners out there. That's when I was looking at my trades and going, "Okay. Well, if anything hits a resistance line, I get that reversal pattern. I'm not going to wait for it to happen. You have to give back some for it to come back to your stop loss. I'm sick of the give back."

That's when I honed in on the aggressive exit strategy. Sometimes, at different times in the market, things will change as well. When you hit that cluster of losses, ask yourself why. Am I doing something wrong here? Am I trading emotionally? Am I not following my trading plan? Is my trading system basically not working right now? What is the market doing? What can I do differently? You need to question yourself as a trader all the time.

In my early days of trading I had what I called a self-awareness journal. I used to write in it at the end of each trade day about how I felt after that trade day. I would record things that I had done in that trade day. I would actually look back at it at the end of the week and write down what I had learned from trading that week. I really learned a lot about myself and my emotions through trading. That's something that I recommend for any new trader starting out, and moms especially. You really need to get to know yourself and your weaknesses as a trader. The thing is not to keep repeating the same mistakes over and over.

Write in a journal; keep the information there. Be aware. Always look back and study your trades. Question everything. The other thing that I would do is run a scan once a quarter and look at it to get a feel for what kind of market we were in. What were the top winning trades of the last quarter? Is there any share out there that rose 50 percent in value or 30 percent in value? Did my system bring them up? Was an entry signal given in there? Yes, I was in one or two of those. Great.

Hopefully, my clients are in some of the other ones. I'm not going to be in every trade. I can't. My portfolio heat won't allow me to. I always believe in studying winning trades and looking at win trades. Where would the trading system have got you into those trades and where would the system have got you out of those trades? It's always about honing that skill. I still run that scan every quarter and look at the top performing shares of the quarter.

I love it when I say to myself, "Yeah, great. I was on that trade." No, I wasn't on that trade, but look, my system bought it up ... I know my system bought it up because I remember seeing it. I obviously didn't enter it for different reasons: maybe my portfolio heat, or maybe I had another option that I chose on that day. You didn't know, my system still would've worked if I was in it. So I'm always studying those winning trades.

Jane: For myself, I have found that if I review my trades every day, it helps immensely.

Justine: You'd be doing a lot more trades than me in one day. The shorter term trader tends to have more trades. I believe that even though my short term trading wasn't successful, it was successful because I learned a lot about myself and I became a better trader from it. Do you know what I mean? Because with long term trading, it takes a lot longer to actually learn about yourself and your weaknesses.

You learn about it very fast when you are day trading. Day trading brings everything up, as you know. All your demons come up. One thing you have to be very conscious of is doing things that I call feel good strategies. You do them in the moment to make you feel good right now, but they're not always the right strategy at the end of the day. You deviate from your trading plan as well. That's what I also call averaging down - a feel good strategy. I never add to any trades when they are going against me. I know that's a question you had: do you add to losers? I only ever add to winning trades.

For me, averaging down is what I call a feel good strategy. You bought into something, maybe at 10 dollars. For me, if it falls to say nine dollars and my stop is hit, I'm out of it. When it goes down to eight dollars, I see people who are like, "My broker is still saying it's a really good share and it's going to go back up, so I'll buy some more. If I buy some more at eight dollars and I average my buy price to nine dollars, it falls to six dollars. It's still going to get back up. It's a really good healthy share. I'll buy some more now and I'll average my buy price down."

That might feel good at the time, and it might be a great strategy if that share does go back up to 10 dollars. But if it doesn't, you have just dug yourself into a way bigger hole. I only add to trades as they're going my way and I will risk my profits to buy more. I never put myself back into a losing situation to add to a trade. My biggest risk on any trade is getting my initial stop loss to break it even. That's the biggest risk.

Once I get a stop loss at break even, I'm just protecting my capital. If I can't get that stop loss to break even in a certain time frame, that's when the time stop kicks in. The biggest risk on the trade is when I first open it and that trade doesn't go my way. When my stop loss is hit, I know that I'm going to lose that amount of money. That's fine. I'm happy to lose that amount of money, and it's freeing my capital up now to put my money into something else that will hopefully be the bigger winner. You never know. You could still have that cluster of losses.

I just see each trade as an opportunity. Even if it's a losing trade, that's just an opportunity now. My capital is free to take on board another trade. I only actually add to winning trades.

Jane: Besides your own book, of course, what other books would you recommend to new traders?

Justine: *Trading in the Zone* by Mark Douglas; *How to Profit in Bull and Bear Markets* by Stan Weinstein; then Tharp's *Trade Your Way to Financial Freedom*. He's written many more books since then. I think his latest one is *Trading Beyond the Matrix*. For me it was his information about money management in *Trade Your Way to Financial Freedom* that I loved. He talks about testing systems like taking somebody who's got a really good system. It's been a long time since I've read the book.

He took a trading system that was working. Then he took a system where he just threw a dart at a dart board and you entered that trade or flipped a coin. It's just a random flip coin system. He found that the entry strategy didn't matter. Both systems performed well if you had the money management rules in there. You cut your losses short, and you stay with the winning trades. At the end of the day, it's the exits that are so important. These are probably my top three books.

Jane: Is there anything else that you would tell a female trader who is new to the industry, just coming in?

Justine: Spend some time writing a trading plan. This is just something that people put off. As a mom, you might have a husband who's bringing in the money. You might feel like you need to bring in the money. The sooner that you can get into the market, the better. Just hold off until you've written that trading plan. The reason why people put it off is they see it as being a really big task, something that's really hard to do, and it is hard work.

You need to get the information out of your head and into a Word document. In my book *Smart Trading Plans* I actually give you a Word document. You just have to fill it in under the headings. There are questions in there throughout my book to help you complete it. Once you get it out of your head and on paper, you free up your mind. It's all in your head. I know how I'm trading; it's all in my head. But once you put it on paper you realize the things that you're missing that you need to spend a bit more time on.

It opens you up to then be able to take on board new information. There's only so much you can keep holding in your head. It's like a weight lifted off your shoulders when you do complete that trading plan. It is a work in progress: don't expect it to be final. You're going to spend time. You will look at your trades at the end of each day and at the end of each week. Ask yourself a question: "Is there anything in here that I need to adjust in my trading plan?" I thought my trading plan was complete. Then 2010 hit and during that consolidation phase, things just weren't working. I introduced an aggressive exit strategy. Things can still change, and when they do, you need to update your trading plan too.

Jane: I feel like the best traders are the ones who have adapted with the changes of the market to figure out how to improve their plan to its best possible form, so it's a winning plan throughout the market changes.

Justine: When something's not working, question it, adapt it to suit, or take a break. You don't have to trade every different kind of market. There can be markets where you say, "No, I'm not comfortable trading short, so I will stay out of the market during a bear market." How do you know you're in a bear market? What's going to define to you that you're in a bear market now, so that you take that break? There might be some markets you aren't comfortable trading at all, and that's when you just need to not be in the market. You can learn during that time. Maybe you will decide to develop a strategy for that kind of market for next time.

I find I became a better trader through teaching. Sharing made me look at myself all the time. I don't think I would have been reflecting on myself so much if I wasn't doing that because you just dismiss it: "Yeah, whatever. Just forget about that." You know what I mean? There's nobody to justify anything to. I believe that sharing made me a better trader, and you probably find the same because you're sharing it too. You're sharing your mistakes; you're sharing... But because you're sharing your mistakes, you're going, "I know I did this. I know next time ..." It really makes you take a good look at yourself all the time and everything that you're doing.

Jane: Definitely. For me, there are certain times in the day when I know that I'm not going to enter. I wait until 9:50 in the morning. I don't enter during the chaos, the panic, at the beginning. The morning panic.

Justine: No, I never used to either when I was day trading. I used to wait until the market opened at 10 and I didn't start trading until after that time. I needed the charts to build up the intra day charts to 10:30, 10:40.

Jane: Yeah, you need to see the direction in which the stock has chosen to move. I also do yoga. To me, trading is very much being present in that moment. Instead of hoping or wanting something to happen, you have to be seeing it happen and then you react to the price movement. I definitely trade the charts. Whatever the catalyst is for major movement, and the large volume, because I'm not going to get into something that's illiquid. It's very much being present in that moment and looking at the charts. For me, I love the tension and watching the level two. I can see when the reverse is setting up. It could be little pull back. It's a point to me; it's a trigger to get out and lock the profit.

Justine: Another book that really helped me is *The Big Leap* by Gay Hendricks. Have you read *The Big Leap*?

Jane: I haven't.

Justine: That was the one that helped supercharge my trading, where "You hit a certain level and then you can sabotage yourself."

Know when you're in your zone of genius. Like you, and me, when you're sitting in front of that computer for 30 minutes and the kids don't interrupt me, I'm just in the zone. It's why I love trading time. He talks about understanding your zone of genius. That's when you work and operate at your best. Your upper limit, that's what he called it.

You've got to understand that when you hit your upper limit, that's when you can actually sabotage yourself. For some people, that's a lot. They do it in relationships, in love: they break up with the person because they don't feel they're worthy of it. In trading, you can do it with the money. You hit a certain point when things come up for you and then you can start sabotaging it. I found *The Big Leap* to be a huge book. I love Eckhart Tolle's *New Earth* and *Living in the Now*. I've done a heap of his work and everything as well.

Jane: Like you mentioned before, I also find that trading is a self-reflection. If you're distracted in your mind, you're probably not going to have the best trade. If you're very centered and you're honest with yourself about everything too, then you're going to be clear and honest with your trades. If it's going against you, you're going to take it as a lesson. If not, you're just going to continue to downgrade yourself in your trades.

Justine: Yeah, I love it that you're on that same mindset, Jane. I don't tell a lot of people about that until they're at a certain level. I just find ... Especially men, they go, "You've got to be kidding me?" Women are a bit more open to the spiritual side of the trading. That's probably why I do enjoy when I get those female clients, because we talk on a more spiritual level than I would with men.

Jane: I think one thing that's very different about a female trader is being more emotional in general, but we also know how to control our emotions better. We've been taught to feel the full range of emotion as women, whereas with a man it's, "Ugh." You know? "This is my ego. It's not going with me; I'm going to get mad. I might revenge trade. I might get back into it and really blow up the account." Whereas a woman might step back, assess it, look at what's going wrong, and learn from it.

Justine: I remember those emotions when I was caught up after the World Trade Center crashed. I did, I had to feel it. I had to give myself those three weeks to get over it. I'm sure that there'd be men out there revenge trading through that.

The only thing that I can't say is I can't guarantee that people will be profitable from trading in any way whatsoever. Under my license and everything I do, I can't say, "Yes, you will make money by doing this." The reality is, not everybody will. Not everybody's personalities can handle it.

Jane: Exactly. Yes, the disclaimer. Anybody that does guarantee you will make money trading is probably a scammer. Wonderful. Well, thank you so much, Justine. I hope you have an amazing day and an amazing week. Thank you so much. I really appreciate the time.

Justine: I should ask you, how did you find me? Being in Canada.

Jane: Just searching on the internet. I was trying to find women who are successful obviously in their trading but who are already out there and want people to know about their success. Thank you so much and thank you for sharing. I've learned a lot from you by listening, and hearing your strategies as well.

Justine: Well, lovely to talk with you.

Jane: Thank you. It was a pleasure, an absolute pleasure. Have a wonderful day.

Justine: You too. Bye.

Stefanie Kammerman

USA

Website: www.thestockwhisperer.com
Twitter: @VolumePrintcess
StockTwits: @The_Stock_Whisperer
YouTube: The Stock Whisperer @ The Java Pit

I found Stefanie through researching *The Money Show* speakers. Stefanie has an interesting trading career that began back in the 1990s in an office of big shot professionals. The necessary discipline to turn it into a successful career was learned from day one as an assistant. She then turned those rules into a home-based profession and is now one of the biggest educators about dark pool prints.

Stefanie: I'm very similar to you. I want to let you know that. I started trading 23 years ago. Before I had kids.

Jane: Okay.

Stefanie: It was later when I was pregnant with my daughter. When I was seven months pregnant I started to have those Braxton Hicks contractions, and I had to stop trading in the office.

Jane: Okay.

Stefanie: I didn't think that it was stressful trading, but I thought you know what? I have to stop. This is not good. I didn't want to go into labor, so I was on bed rest. I thought I could do all this from home, and trade from home. No. Not in 1998. We didn't have the tools then that we have now. I got into the music business, and then in about 2009, you know, my kids were older; I had two kids by then.

Jane: Mm-hmm.

Stefanie: I said, you know, I need to do something that I can do from home, because I want to be there when my kids get off the bus. But being a mother was of course number one priority. That's how I got involved on the online trading. I said, you know, I was trading, but I was lonely.

Jane: Yes.

Stefanie: Here I was, trading by myself on a laptop. I was making money, but it was boring. I saw this online trading room, and I thought, wow, this is so amazing. This is like being back in my old trading room. I have all these people that share the same passion as me, because none of my girlfriends understood anything about the stock market. I was really thirsty to meet other people who traded and had the same passion. It was instantly amazing. I found this great group of traders; I became really popular. Everybody wanted to know my secrets.

Jane: For sure. Now, what was the trading room that you used?

Stefanie: I was in Cyber Trading University. It was actually through a neighbor of mine. I met him at a birthday party. I knew he was involved in online trading, and so I went up to him, and I said, "What exactly do you do? I'm intrigued," and he said, "I run this online trading room." I said, "Really? I used to work at Schoenfeld Securities." And he said, "Really?" He was so impressed, number one that I was a woman: "Oh my God, you're a woman, and you worked at this biggest Schoenfeld firm in New York."

Jane: Right.

Stefanie: And he said, "You've got to come to my room," and he gave me free access, and he supplied me with some day trading software, and I said, "Okay." I joined it, and I loved it, instantly. I said, "This is really great," and I became popular really fast there. I just started to input my trades, what I was doing, and everybody wanted to learn from me. I started to teach classes. Maybe 50 people would sign up for my classes at that time.

Jane: Wow.

Stefanie: No sales people were necessary. They just all called up, "We want to take Stefanie's workshop." He said, "Can you do another one?" I did another one, and another one. Before I knew it, I was running; I was doing everything.

Jane: Wow.

Stefanie: I was running around, and I built it from 20 people to over 200 people. Then, I kind of got too big. I'll leave it at that. Where I became very, very popular and I was politically pushed out, which I would have done the

161

same thing if it was my place, I guess. It was the best thing that ever happened, because I started my own. I met Larry Berman. Are you familiar with Larry?

Jane: No. I don't know Larry.

Stefanie: He's on BNN. In fact, was I in Quebec? Where was I? I was on tour with him for three years.

Jane: Awesome.

Stefanie: All across Canada. Yeah. He's on BNN. He has a show every Monday called *Berman's Call*. He's the biggest portfolio manager in Canada. I think he's managing a billion dollars, right now. I met him in Vancouver, when I was there at Money Show a couple of years back. I didn't even know who he was. I just went up to him, and I said, "I'm doing a presentation, in an hour. You should come, and I promise I'm going to teach you something." He said, "Do you know who I am?" I said, "No. Who are you?" He said, "I'm the Jim Cramer of Canada." I said, "Oh. It's very nice to meet you. I'm the Jim Cramer of New York," and I was just making a joke.

Jane: Right.

Stefanie: There was a big poster, Jane, outside of him. I'm a little ditsy, sometimes. I didn't even notice it. He was actually leaving with his computer. He had just done an enormous presentation there, which I hadn't seen, and here I was coming up to him, and he was like, "Oh. Yeah. Let me check that girl out; she thinks she can teach me something, today." He did. He came, and he was really impressed. He goes, "I don't do what you do because I run a billion dollars, but what you do makes sense and I'd love to work with you one day." And he put me on a six-month interview where he challenged me in ways nobody had ever done. He'd say, "Okay. What are you seeing today?" and I'd say, "Larry, I see this huge sale print on FXI (China ETF) they're selling in China."

Jane: Yeah.

Stefanie: "Really? I just bought some a couple of days ago." "Well, they're selling it," and FXI would go down, and then he would say, "What are you seeing today?" and here and there. After six months of interrogation, no, it was actually an interview, he said, "Come on, you can come on my tour." This was really the big break for me, because he's huge. He just has huge audiences, like 500 people, and he packs the room. I did three tours across Canada. I have a lot of traders that are up in Canada, so for me it was a win-win situation. I got to meet everybody.

Jane: That's wonderful.

Stefanie: They've become my family. I mean, I've been trading with the same group for years, and of course it keeps growing, and growing. I'll tell you that I'm a huge inspiration for women.

Jane: Yeah.

Stefanie: So many women come to me, because they think, if she can do it, I can do it. Now, when I look out in the audience, there are a lot more women than there were when I first started.

Jane: That's great.

Stefanie: It's great. Yeah. I love it. These women are really great traders. I don't look at it as women versus men. I'll be honest. You're either disciplined and you can trade, or you're not disciplined and you're not going to make it in this business. Discipline is the most important aspect of trading. People get wiped out. It's usually one trade that wipes them out.

Jane: I agree.

Stefanie: Definitely. You know? It's okay. It's not about right or wrong. It's nothing to do with you in the trade; it's either a successful trade, or it's an unsuccessful trade. There's no such thing as a loser; there are no losers and winners. It's an unsuccessful trade or a successful trade. I know one of your questions you had asked me is do you add to a loser, no. But when you add to an unsuccessful trade, you become a loser.

Jane: Mm-hmm (affirmative).

Stefanie: Okay? That's the difference. I expect losing trades, every single day. I expect it, and I teach that to my traders. It didn't work out and this is what I'm risking. I'm risking $50 to make $500.

Jane: For sure.

Stefanie: For me, those are great. Those are great option trades. I call them lottery tickets. I took one on Apple recently, where I bought very cheap calls when Apple was at $92.00, and it hit my target of 100, pre-market, this morning, and I doubled. It was a small risk, and a very big reward. It's really what I teach, of course, to expect losers. When you don't expect a loser, you don't know how to handle it when it comes. Everybody has a trade that just doesn't work out, and it could be news-related. It could be we didn't enter properly, all that stuff.

It's about how you handle those trades that don't work out, because those are my best trades, by the way. I don't sit there and gloat, "Oh. My God. I made blah, blah, blah," because it has nothing to do with money. I'm happy when I get out of an unsuccessful trade, and I only lose a little bit of money. Those are my best trades.

Jane: Okay.

Stefanie: Every single day.

Jane: It's satisfying to see that you got out before you had a big loss.

Stefanie: Yes. We're just mapping it out first. For me, it's okay. Look, I took a trade on Boeing yesterday. I bought the calls, the 129 calls, and it hit. I got out. I like to scale out of trades, so I scaled out of half yesterday, then when it popped up this morning to $129.75, I got out of the other half. It's down, and that's great. If it breaks above 130, I'll take another trade, but it's about mapping it out before you get in, knowing when you're going to get out. Most people don't do that. They get in a trade and go, "Okay, Stef, where should I get out?" I'm like, "You have to know that."

Jane: Before you even enter.

Stefanie: Yes. Especially with options, because they'll turn on you. You have to get out into strength and they'll turn on you really, really quickly. You have to go like a robot, with no emotion whatsoever.

Jane: Now, when you first started trading, Stefanie, back 23 years ago, did you have any mentors or anyone you looked up to?

Stefanie: Yes. My first day, I'm going to tell you, I didn't know anything about the stock market. I was very young. I was 24 years old, and I needed a job. I got a job as an assistant to one of the best traders at Schoenfeld Securities, and I was in a million-dollar room. Those guys, I'm going to be honest, were my mentors. I mean, these guys were successful; they were making millions of dollars a year, right in front of me. I'll be honest. I asked my boss, I said, "Look. What book should I read? I don't know anything about the market. I need that one book that's really going to point me in the right direction." And he told me, *Reminiscences of a Stock Operator*. It's by Edwin Lefèvre, and it's the Jesse Livermore story.

Jane: I know it.

Stefanie: That book is my Bible. Jesse Livermore, a tape reader, used to get kicked out of those bucket shops. There are so many great lines in that book. Everything like that, last eighth, is the most expensive eighth in the world. I live by that every day. If my target's 100, I'm getting out before a 100. I'm not going to go hold out for a 100. I'm getting out at $99.75, which is exactly what happened to Apple, yesterday; it went right there and then pulled back down again. There are so many great things, and he is Jessie Livermore. I'll be honest; he's my mentor. That book was written in 1923. Nothing has changed. Everything that he lived by is, oh, my God, the psychology is amazing. Reading the tape, for me, is the only way to trade. I don't know any other way that's going to give me better results than actually looking at the tape, and following the big prints, the big trades, especially the dark pool.

Jane: Mm-hmm (affirmative).

Stefanie: That's my secret. I've called the last 10 corrections before they happened on social media. I'm not psychic, I'm not; I just know how to spot when the big guys are selling. I take pictures, I teach, I educate, and I put it out there on the internet to teach people. Every day I get thank yous. For example, I just spotted a seven-and-a-half million share print, the dark pool trade on Apple at $99.16. Then I spotted a five million, same exact level, $99.16. What I like to do is wait for the end of the day to see which side. If it closes below $99.00, I'm going to turn bearish.

Jane: Ok.

Stefanie: If it closes above $99.50, I'll have a 100; I'm going to even turn more bullish. I'll put a new trade on it. I'm sitting here waiting to see which side of the line it's going to close on. Now, if I'm not sure at the end of today, I'm not going to get in a trade. I don't need to be the first person in. I just know a gigantic trade is being done and whichever side of the line it falls on I'm going to take it. I'll go long here; I'll go short. I'm prepared in both directions. Sometimes I get it wrong at first, but I'll get out. I'll reverse. But for the most part, I'm going to tell you it's amazing just following these big trades. And that is my secret. Following the volume.

Jane: Of course, because you want to work with momentum instead of against it.

Stefanie: Right. I mean, I'll go against. Look, there are traders out there who come into my room: they're so rebellious. They don't want to go with the trend. I know I'm going to find that bottom. I want to find that top. Okay. I get it, but show me a big print. Show me that seller at the top. That could be today; that could be the seller that is selling today that bought it at 90. We had a very big volume around that area, or 92.50 there was big volume. That's where I went long on the 16th; on May 16th there was a huge volume that day.

It was the first day that Apple closed on the daily chart above the 8 EMA. For me, high above average volume closing across the eight is a huge momentum change signal that it's turning bullish. It had a fantastic run, went to 100, but here's this big volume at the top near resistance. I'm going to wait it out and see if it closes below it, or of course above it, or it could be ready for another run up. Again, I'm keeping an open mind. The overall market is definitely showing a little weakness today.

Jane: Definitely. Now, when you go into a trade, are you typically in one trade at a time, or do you-

Stefanie: No.

Jane: Okay. How many do you typically trade at once?

Stefanie: I could be in 30 trades right now, or I could have longer term swing trades on.

Jane: Okay.

Stefanie: I have short-term, overnight trades, and then I have day trades.

Jane: Okay.

Stefanie: I got 30 things going on.

Jane: I hear you. I do a little bit of it all, too.

Stefanie: Yeah. You know. Different, but you have to have that. It was difficult, when I went from just swing trading in, 2009, how many years-

Jane: Seven years.

Stefanie: Yeah. I started to learn how to day trade, which I used to think was crazy. How do these people do it? My friend, I love it.

Jane: Out of curiosity, how old were your kids when you went into day trading?

Stefanie: In 2009, my son was nine, and my daughter was 11.

Jane: Okay.

Stefanie: Yeah.

Jane: They were both in school.

Stefanie: Yeah. Good ages. How old are your kids?

Jane: I just have one daughter, and she is 22 months.

Stefanie: Just a baby.

Jane: Yeah.

Stefanie: That's cute. Mine is going to college next year. It happens fast. That's kind of hard, you have to trade around the naptime.

Jane: She's actually, thankfully, in daycare. She absolutely loves it, so it buys me time during the day. I learned not to trade when she was home. I would schedule her naps at the market open, so that I would have 45 minutes to an hour of time, but then I found it was just too difficult to juggle both of them. I wanted to give her the priority. I said, once she goes into daycare, then I will commit full-time dedication to trading.

Stefanie: Right. Definitely. Yes. Once they were good in school, because it's hard. When they were babies I took some time off from work. I was very fortunate. I'll be honest; I did extremely well my first couple of years trading, only because I didn't trade right away. I didn't even think I was going to be a trader. Here I was in this million-dollar-room; these guys were teaching me how to trade.

I'll tell you my first lesson: it's not about the money. My boss was up like $20,000.00 in the first 20 minutes of trading, and he started to get upset, and he's cursing, his fist is hitting the desk, he threw a chair across the room, and I thought, what is wrong? My first day, what is wrong with you? I'm looking at his PNR going, he's up $20,000.00; what, are you insane? I would die to make $20,000.00 in 20 minutes. He said, "It's not about the money." I go, "Okay." He said, "It's because I lost my discipline. I shouldn't have sold Intel. I don't care if I made money on it; I lost my discipline. Next time I'll get crushed." Because I was his assistant, and he was a really nice guy, he just lost it, because he had lost his discipline. I said, "Just tell me what the rules are. Just tell me the rules, and I'm going to make sure that you trade out of everything perfectly, because I don't want any more chairs flying in this room." So he did. It was so simple. It was okay, because it was fractions back then. Three quarters off the low on my shorts, I'm getting out. Three quarters of the high on my longs, I'm getting out. I said, "Perfect. That's it; I'm going to be in charge, now." I was. I held all those positions, anytime, anything was okay. Scotty, Microsoft is three quarters off the low, get out. Microsoft is three quarters off the high, get out. It was like that.

All day long, and I was trading for him. I said, "Okay. What are the conditions that you get into the stocks?" He told me them and I said, "Okay." Every day at the end of the day was swing trading. I said, "Okay. This one, that one, this one, that one." I never thought about the money. I was a robot. I thought I just didn't want to see Scotty lose it.

I said, "This is what you've got to do." We switched to another firm called Onsite Trading, because they offered us lower commissions. Then he decided, "I'm going to move to Florida, because I don't want to pay New York state tax."

I said, "Oh. God. What am I going to do?" I cannot move to Florida. The firm, Onsite Trading said, "You know what you're doing. You were trained by the best. We're going to give you a quarter of a million dollars."

Jane: Nice.

Stefanie: I was the first female trader.

Jane: Very nice.

Stefanie: Yeah. I worked with 100 men. I never even thought about that. I'm going to be honest; it didn't even hit me that I was working with all men, until the Christmas party. Okay? Because there I was and no other women were invited to it.

Jane: Ah-ha.

Stefanie: No spouses.

Jane: Right.

Stefanie: It was me and 100 drunk men. That's when it hit me. I'm in a room, and it's like they're swirling around me, and they're all drinking, and I'm going, "Oh. My God. Now, I feel like a woman." I had never felt like a woman until that moment, oh, my God. I actually had to go outside. I thought, I have to get outside. It was a little uncomfortable. When I was at work, they were like my brothers. I was one of the guys, and I was running the trading desk, and in my first year I won trader of the year.

Jane: Great.

Stefanie: I did really, really well. I'm going to tell you, it's because I did not think. I did not think about money. I didn't think about anything, but am I following these rules? It's the only way I knew how to trade and how to do this. I saw success. It was just easy for me. It wasn't really until I got pregnant, of course, like I told you. I had to leave, and I thought I could do it from home. I couldn't do it from home. I ended up going into the music business for a while, which was really good. I'm still in the music business. It just doesn't pay very well, but I love it. I write music for television, background, jingles, that kind of stuff.

Jane: Very nice.

Stefanie: I just don't have time to devote to it right now, because I started my business, and this is really taking over. Trading and running a trading room keep me disciplined. People say, "How do you stay disciplined?" Everybody is seeing what I'm doing, I'm calling out everything, and I have to be disciplined. If I'm not disciplined, somebody in my room will call me out. Yeah. They'll say, "Stefanie, what are you doing? That's breaking your rules." It keeps mein line. I love it. I call my trades, okay, I'm buying it here, this is my target, this why I'm getting out. All that stuff.

Jane: That's great.

Stefanie: Yeah. It's the only way. Or else I could see how you could lose your discipline.

Jane: When you started, you had your rules from your first boss, Scotty. Do you still use the same rules today?

Stefanie: I do. I use many of the rules, but I've gotten much pickier. Things have changed a little bit, and I've learned a lot. I learned not just from those guys in the beginning, but I have also learned from all the traders that I've come in contact with over the years. It's a process. We're always learning. Traders come in my room, I teach them stuff, they teach me stuff. "Stef, check this out," and I'll go, "Wow that's amazing." I want to put everything together, and use that.

I always tell people, "If it's working, stick with it; but if it's not, then you want to lose that. I'll give you something that's so much better. If this indicator is working for you, that's great. Continue on that, but check this out: this is really great, too." I've recently added futures. I watch the futures a lot, and the pivots with that. I think that they're fantastic. I watch the E-mini's in conjunction with the SPY and the prints. I like a lot of things kind of in conjunction, working together.

Jane: It's all harmonious. It all works together, and it all flows together, so if you're following all of that, it makes sense with everything else.

Stefanie: Yeah. When everything lines up, I mean, that's when I go in bigger. I'm very conservative. I'll go in small, small, but when I see everything lining up, like the gold trade we spotted back in January, we spotted the biggest prints on iShares Gold Trust, IAU, and I posted it up on StockTwits and Twitter. We're going on 10 million shared bought.

Jane: Wow.

Stefanie: And I said, "This is the bottom. The gold coma is over." I was tweeting like a maniac; we went in big. That feed, I'm going to be honest, a lot of times it's just one trade, that's it. That's all you need for the year. It was humongous, but we waited a long time for that setup to happen, for the rounded bottom, and the big guys to come in with those big blocks. Also, it's like a W pattern on the bottom.

You need volume. Volume is key. When you don't have volume, they can fake you out; they can do so many things if you don't have volume. When you have technicals lining up and then you see the dark pool trades coming in, it was like holy shit, this is amazing. We did really, really well on that.

Jane: I have a question for you. What do you mean by dark pool trade?

Stefanie: Okay. Forty percent of all the trades that are being done right now are being done in an alternate exchange called the dark pool; it's been around since the beginning of time. It used to be the upstairs room. When I first started trading they put me in front of this machine called Instinet Machine. It was a green glowing machine and there was a dark pool exchange. I got to see where all the big guys were buying and selling.

We didn't do any order until we checked the Instinet. Where's the big guy? Goldman-Sachs started hiding all his stuff in the dark pool.

Jane: Okay.

Stefanie: Because we were all watching him. It used to be really easy to trade. Just watch where's Goldman? Is he on a bid? Is he on the offer? Then, he started to hide it, he hid it on the ECN Books, and he hid it in the dark pool. Now, okay, those machines were like $20,000.00 a month to have, and if you were at a big firm, you had access to it. When I went home, thinking I could trade, I was like, no way. I don't have a dark pool. I have nothing.

Jane: Right.

Stefanie: I have dial-up on AOL. I think I'll just have some babies and do the baby thing for a while, and then come back to trading at a later date, which is really what happened. Everything changed. When I started in that online trading room, I started to see things in my time and sales with the software that I was using. I was given DAS Trader Pro to use and it has dark pool data feed.

Jane: Okay.

Stefanie: The exchange is FADF on mine. Now, I don't know what you're using, but it could be ATTN, ADFN. It depends on whatever software you have. Now, some software doesn't have dark pool data feed. If you don't have the dark pool data, you are completely blind to what's going on. You're missing 40%. A guy from a big software company came to me and said, "All our software is so much better than what you're using." And so he gave me a trial, and I saw that he didn't even have dark pool data feed. I said, "You guys are missing out. Really? You're not seeing this trade. We went over trade for trade." I go, "You're not seeing this, you're not seeing that, you're not seeing this, you're missing everything." I hopefully changed his program. I said, "All your scanners are off; everything's off, because you don't have 40% of volume that's being done." I have Charles Schwab. If you can get Charles Schwab, this thing will change your life. Okay? It's the Block, it's free. You can open an account with $50.00, and tell them you'll fund it at another time. I only keep $50.00 in it, because the commissions are high, but I use it strictly for their dark pool data feed. It gives me all the big trades. I've scanned it across the entire market.

In the block trades what I really use it for is the late prints. In every correction that I've spotted, before it happened, I spotted the big guys selling in the dark pool and hiding their orders until the next day.

Jane: Okay.

Stefanie: I see these late sell prints coming across, the SPY wasn't trading at 210 it would be down at 208, and all of a sudden I'd see this big sell print coming in at 210 all day long, like millions, and I always thought that's illegal, how do they do that? Those trades were done yesterday. I learned from a floor trader who said, "Oh. Yeah. They do a trade in London, they cross it with their New York desk, and they don't have to report that trade until the next day." That's how they hide freaking 30 million shares. So we keep track; we're obsessed. My trading room is obsessed with the dark pool. We count them. One girl in my room counts them all. We know where they are.

We know all the big levels going back to last year. That's how I spot. When I see three days in a row of the dark pool selling, hiding their orders, and of course we see five prints on the VXX, the fear, that's when I call corrections.

Jane: Ok.

Stefanie: It's been right 10 for 10. It just makes sense, because if you're the big guys, how are you going unload 10 million shares, 20 million shares without moving the market down?

Jane: Of course.

Stefanie: They hide it. Yeah. It's so manipulative. They do this when they buy, as well. When we know when a correction is over, we see them buying it, hiding it, and reporting it the next day. I see a lot of weird stuff, Jane. Okay? I saw, before the bombs went off in Brussels in the airport.

Jane: Yeah.

Stefanie: We spotted the biggest buy prints on TVIX. That's the fear TF, the day before. I've never seen such good trades.

Jane: Wow.

Stefanie: We didn't know what was going on; we are like, "Why the big fear? Who's scared right now? Something's going to happen in the market." The next day I come in, put the news on, and I'm like terrorism in the airport, and I go, "Oh. My God. That was a terrorist." Who else would know about that? Who else would be making these big trades?

Jane: Yeah.

Stefanie: Nobody knew that was going to happen on the fear index, unless you were connected with the terrorists. Whoever knew was trying to profit off of it. I don't think they made much money, because the market was down and then it went back up and bounced. I don't know if maybe there was another plan on US soil that got changed.

Jane: Yeah.

Stefanie: Or something like that. There were actually two: there was that one and there was another one in a park or something the next day. It freaked me out. I see insider trading before it happens, all the time. I see big block trades, and I'm like, we saw a big trade on Amazon once. We usually never see a big trade like this on Amazon, and then 30 minutes later, the news came out, and the thing skyrocketed. It's really, for me, the only way to trade.

Jane: For scanning, you would say you use the dark pool trading mostly, or you don't use anything else? I mean, it sounds like that's your primary source for finding your Stocks to trade.

Stefanie: It is. It's my primary source. I also use TC2000.

Jane: Okay.

Stefanie: Which I used to scan above the 8 EMA, and below the 8 EMA. I like the first day with above average volume. You have Trend Change, and that works really, really well. I love that. It's a great scanner. It's always about volume. I'm very technical. I draw trend lines. I find that exact spot on the chart where the trend changes from up to down, down to up. We're trading against computers. It's so technical. I have the television on mute. Really, the whole day. I don't care. I don't want to hear what they're saying. I like to see that news is coming out, but I don't want to hear their take on it and what the market should do, because that's horrible. They're always coming up with 10 reasons why it's up. Why is it down? No. We hit a technical resistance, so sellers came in and now we're going down. You want to find a reason for that? Okay. Go ahead.

Jane: The computers did it.

Stefanie: Yeah. I keep it on because I just like to know when oil numbers are coming out, or when this is coming out, and that, but it's on mute.

Jane:	That's what you really use for your news sources? The TV screen on mute?
Stefanie:	Right. Exactly.
Jane:	Very nice. Now, when do you start your trading? Do you start it the day before, at market close?
Stefanie:	Six a.m. Six o'clock; I'll be up. Sometimes I'll be up at four. If I'm up at 4 a.m., I'll be at my computer, there's volume, there's trading going on. I watch the futures. I start very early. As early as I can. I look for pre market volume. That's my secret. Making my whispers, this morning. I put out a free YouTube video, it's free. It's called the Whisper of Day. This is where I call out my hot day trading stocks for the day. Today's whisper was Abercrombie. My traders did really well.
Jane:	I was just looking at the reversal on Abercrombie right now.
Stefanie:	Yes. Twenty-two is my level. If it broke below that this morning, very bearish.
Jane:	Short it.
Stefanie:	Yeah. Or, if it broke above $22.55, it was a good long. There was actually a pop at the beginning. I'll be honest: I don't trade for the first 15 minutes the market's open. That's a shakeout period. I wait 15 minutes, then wherever it is, I watch for the levels.
Jane:	I do the same thing.
Stefanie:	Yeah. See, you're smart. It's shaky. If I'm going in a swing trade, though, I'll get out.
Jane:	On a pop up.

Stefanie: Yeah. Or, even pre-market, if they pop it up on small volume, I'll get out, and I'll use that to my advantage, but for day trading, no. Absolutely not. Yeah. My secret is volume. We were watching oil this morning, but I was only bullish on USO, so above $12.20.

That's the big level of a trend line. It's also another level, and it went up to 12.12, and came down, so that was a no trade. Of course, move on to something else. It's just an example of what we do in my trading room. It's a free video I put out every morning. It's a 93% success rate. Which is crazy.

Jane: Very nice.

Stefanie: Over two years I've been doing it, and I never thought I'd be that successful. I just thought, okay, let's do a whisper of the day. My hot stock pick, after three months, oh, wow, it's doing really well. After six months, a year, I said, okay, I think this is great, and it's free. There are a lot of people that just watch it. They get trade ideas; they learn a lot from it. Thanking me. Then, if people really want to learn how I do it, they come into my trading room. They see me doing it every morning, and they see us trading it every day.

Jane: Now, in your trading room, do you do a live screen as well, or is it just the-

Stefanie: Yes.

Jane: Chat room. Okay.

Stefanie: It's my screen.

Jane: Okay.

Stefanie: I share. I draw trend lines. It's really an educational room. I wanted a room where I could teach, while the market is live and open, because it's how I learn. I learned by sitting next to really good traders, and they're teaching me as they're trading. I wanted to do that and give back. I had some really good people teach me, and it's not just that. By me teaching these people in my room, I have incredible traders in there. Some of them are just insane.

We've all learned from each other. We're all calling great stuff out, all day, and we're helping each other. It helps me become a better trader. They see things I didn't see; they call out. I make money on those trades. It's like having this giant trading table, but it's online. I can have 1,000 people if I want to have 1,000 people there. As many people as I can train.

Now, some people just do their own thing in the room. Some people trade exactly the way I do, and some people have their own style. It's all very respectful if you say, "You know what? That's not my style, or that is my style." But I always say paper trade. It takes time to learn. When people come in, and they want to know and learn and do this in two minutes, it's like, "No. I got to make money. I got a family to support." I tell them, "Then, go get a job."

Jane: Yeah.

Stefanie: Because I never say that learning how to trade is easy. I make it look like it's easy, because I've been doing it for so long, but I work my butt off. You know? To learn this, train, experience, psychological control. I was a psychology major in college. I love psychology, but I just didn't want to be a clinical psychologist. I see that there's so much psychology involved in trading. You know that. Right?

Jane: Yeah. I see it's a reflection of yourself and the market, and how you trade.

Stefanie: Right. There are people who self-sabotage themselves. That goes really deep. I work with an amazing lady; her name is Andrea Wieland. This woman, I mean, she helps traders deal with self-sabotage. She goes deep into their childhood, things that happened that they're not even aware of, and it's coming out into their trading. I cannot go that deep. I can help with rules, but there are people who won't listen to me. I do a class called Bootcamp four times a year, and the first rule is no trading. Not even paper trade. There's no live, real trading in this class.

On our very first class this trader broke this rule on the first day by saying, "Oh, I'm trading NUGT." He was trading gold, and I was like, "What are you doing?" "No, but I made money." And I go, "I don't care that you made money; it's all about following rules, and if you cannot follow my rules in this class, you're going to have a really hard time trading." That messed him up the entire time. He was all messed up, because he had broken that rule. Psychology.

Jane: It is.

Stefanie: It's so important. People don't realize. I don't care if you make or lose; I just want to see you follow rules. That's it. Years ago, it was one of my first Bootcamp classes, and I said, "Okay. We're doing a trading competition." On the last day of class, I said, "Okay, you guys take the rules I taught you. I want you to use them. Whoever makes the most money is going to win a prize." Now, let me just tell you: the truth is they were doing so well all week, but all of a sudden, they forgot everything. They were trading in the first 10 minutes. They were choosing stocks they shouldn't be trading, they would go against the trend, crazy stuff.

They all lost money. I was so upset. I remember it was a day trading thing, so this was during lunch. I had to leave my house. I left, and I thought, "What am I going to do?" I had just spent all week, and put forth so much energy teaching these traders, and they all went nuts, and they broke every rule. They lost money. It was a week wasted. Then, I said, "You know what? It's my fault." I said to them, "It's a competition, and whoever makes the most money wins." In their brain it was all about money.

I went back, and I said, "Okay, you guys. It's my fault that you didn't respect the rules, and you lost money. We're going to this again. We're going do it again on Monday. I'm extending the class, and we're doing this. It's not going to be a competition; it's going to be a challenge. Okay? A challenge to follow the rules. I don't care if you make money or you don't make money; everybody can win. All you have to do is stick with my trading rules, and you'll win a prize."

Guess what? They all stuck with the rules, and they all made money. I think, two out of 15 didn't, they were flat, but everybody else did really, really well. They were like, "Wow. I cannot believe it. Oh. My God. You're right. You don't think about money; you got to follow the rules. It works." It was the biggest life-changing moment for many of them. Many people in that class are still with me. They're like, "Wow." Now, it's always a challenge.

Jane: What are your top rules?

Stefanie: For day trading, I actually have a checklist. Where is it? I mean, I've memorized it pretty much, but I gave it to my traders. The first rule is, it has to have 100,000 shares, pre-market. You have to see where the big guys are buying and selling, where they're lined up. Number two, you cannot trade for the first 10 minutes. I like 15, but you can go in after 10. Number three, you have to pick stocks that are under $40.00 to day trade.

If you trade stocks that are over 40, options, okay, I don't like to risk four cents to make 20. That's it. I'm risking four to make 20 or more. You cannot risk four cents on a stock that's really expensive. Right? That's a big shakeout move. There are plenty of stocks that are under 20. Right? I stick with the lower-priced stocks that have a lot of volume. Penny spreads. I don't trade anything penny. I don't trade biotechs. No biotechs are allowed. They get halted. I've seen my best friends get wiped out trading biotechs. The trend is really important. For example, if you're going to go long, it has to be up on the day above where it closed yesterday. It has to be above the 8 EMA on the daily chart. I like it to be close to the 8, because that's a support level. If it's just sitting on top of that 8 EMA, it's amazing. Your risk is so small, and the reward is huge. That really is my biggest secret. Now, if it's really far away from the 8, it's gone up, up, up. Your risk is so much higher that it's going to come back and retrace there, so I'm not going to pick those stocks.

Jane: What chart are you looking at? Are you looking at one minute, two minute, five minute, daily-

Stefanie: I use a daily chart for that 8 EMA where it has to be above it for the longer term trend. Then I look at a five-minute chart. Most of the day, I'm on a five. I'll look in pre-market on a one-minute, or a two-minute, just to see where most of the volume has occurred.

For most of the day, I keep it on a five- minute. Now, I have a SPY chart that I use where I have a five-minute, 15, 30, 60. I like to look at longer time frames on that for more of a bigger swing, but generally I really love five minutes. For me, it's less shake out, and stocks move well on half an hour movements.

That five really shows you that rounded top, and that rounded bottom effect. Yeah. The trend is my rule. I like to compare stocks with ETF's, so if I'm trading Bank of America, I want XLF to also be bearish or bullish along with it. All that same stuff. We see prints. My last rule is really prints. You can break every single rule I just gave you for a big print. If everything is going in one direction, and you see a gigantic print, for example on Apple, then you can break the rules.

Right now, Apple is above it. If it was going against the trend, all that stuff, and you have this big print, you can go long, you can go against the trend, as long as you're staying with the print. It's pretty simple. Those are the rules, but people love to break them. I give my traders in my Bootcamp class emotional stability tests to take to see where they fall on the emotional scale, because traders who are very emotional have a hard time with it.

Jane: Yeah. It's all about self-discipline too, because if you're emotional, then you're probably not disciplined with your emotions.

Stefanie: Right. Pilots do really well. Military. No. People in the military.

Jane: I know. I'm a pilot. That's why.

Stefanie: You are? Because you have a checklist.

Jane: Yeah.

Stefanie: You know, and you stick with that checklist.

Jane: And, you know how to do a scan as well with instruments. You're used to scanning multiple screens really quickly.

Stefanie: And, trust your instruments. Right. Yeah. Exactly. You make a great, great trader. I always say pilots are good. Military. If you're a person who's impulsive, it's not going to be good. There's a whole lot of psychology. I always say, if I have a room of 100 people in a class, and I teach them the rules, I'm going to tell you that only five to seven, maybe 10 at the most, will follow my rules. The other people are going to have a hard time. A lot of people just don't like to follow rules. They have a hard time, or they think "What does she know?" You know, you get that.

Jane: Yes.

Stefanie: Gosh, I get that a lot. I get people that come to me, they're like, "You know, Stefanie," and I don't charge a lot, Jane, for my class. I have no sales people. I have nothing; it's me. Personally, I just like to cover my bandwidth. It costs money to have a room, and have all the software and have all this stuff, and I just like to cover my stuff and make it affordable. But a lot of people come to me and they're like, "You know, Stefanie, gosh, I just paid $20,000.00 for this guy's class, and it wasn't good. Can you just give me a class for free?" I'm like, "You know, I'm sorry."

Jane: There are no free lunches. Sorry.

Stefanie: I don't charge a lot, but it took me 300 hours, seriously, to put my workshop together. It's very time-consuming. It's not a lot. "No, but I don't want to spend any more money, and if I just make money trading, then I'll buy your class," and I'm like, "That's just not the way it works." I get this a lot. You'd be shocked. It's like, "Maybe you should get a job doing something else." It's just I do get that, and I'm not sure if I was a guy they would have said that or not, not quite sure.

Jane: Yeah.

Stefanie: It is what it is.

Jane: Definitely. Now, it's interesting, you don't have anything on your rules that talks about risk management, really. I mean, besides your 8 EMA. Right?

Stefanie: Stop losses. No. Stop loss is big. You have to have a stop loss; you have to map out your trades. Sorry, I missed that one. It is on my checklist. You have to map out your trade before, again, I risk four cents to make 20.

Jane: Okay. It's one to five.

Stefanie: Yeah. That's on a day trade. If you do everything right, I expect that seven out of 10 are going to work out. If my first three trades are unsuccessful, I stop trading. I'm done, because it's either me or the market. There are days when the market is horrible, and I'm done. It's very shaky. Very small movements. When there's no trend in the overall market-

Jane: It's flat.

Stefanie: Yeah. We had that on Monday. Monday was horrific.

Jane: I had an amazing day. Side note.

Stefanie: You did?

Jane: Yeah.

Stefanie: No. I had a great day yesterday.

Jane: It was a swing trade.

Stefanie: Okay. What were you swinging?

Jane: I swung CLRB and ENDP.

Stefanie: I don't do biotechs. Personally, I cannot do that, because I feel so out of control. That's how I feel when I'm trading a biotech stock. It's that I don't have control; it gets halted. They get halted a lot. All of a sudden you're in it, and all of a sudden it's halted, and now you're gambling. It could go up, it could go down. Just me personally, I'll trade LABU that's L-A-B-U. That's the Direxion biotech, three times the speed. If I like the technicals in the whole sector that's not going to get halted, LABU. Something like that I would trade, but to pick an individual one, for me, but then again, look, you know I'm ultraconservative, and I respect that. I have traders in my room that trade biotechs and that's fine. They know the risk, as long as I tell them the risk, and they're fine, and they do great, but me personally, I'm extremely conservative. I stick with very conservative stocks. That's why I'm still doing it 23 years later.

I actually saw guys that were so good, they were really good traders, and when they got in the biotech stock they got halted, and what did they do? Went down $5.00, they bought more. Okay? Then, it got halted again, and it went down. They bought more, and then they were wiped out. When I saw that happen to my friends, I vowed that I will never trade a biotech stock. I'll stick with software, hardware, gold, silver, or anything but biotech. Just watching that is why I'm so strong on that, but my traders know that. Look, they can do it. That's totally fine. Go ahead, you were asking something about a trading journal?

Jane: Yeah. I was going to ask if you recommend that to any of your students.

Stefanie: Absolutely. They should have a trading journal, especially when they're learning. A lot of times I'll analyze trades, and I'll say, "You know what? You shouldn't even have been in this trade. By not being in this trade, you would have been in a better trade," or, "You did everything right, the trade just didn't work out." It's important to go through them, and also certain times of the day. We don't trade during lunch, so after 11 you don't day trade. Then, again starting at two o'clock, the momentum starts to build up, but the best trades really are from 3:35 and the last 25 minutes. That's it. Unless there's a big print, or something big is happening, other than that sit and wait. But if you saw those big Apple prints and you went long when they broke above, that's okay. Then, you can break the rule for that. Yeah. Journaling is great: this way they can see and check next to it, okay, I did everything right, it just didn't work out. Or why didn't this work out? You learn from that.

People don't paper trade long enough. I say, you paper trade until you're successful for six weeks in a row. Six weeks. If you can do it six week in a row, then you start with small share size. Okay. You start with a 100 shares. If you can make money successfully with 100 shares for two weeks, then you can move up to 200 shares. If you can do that, move up to 400 shares. We all have a threshold where we become uncomfortable in the trade.

Learn where your threshold is, because you start doing silly stuff. Oh. My God. You got nerve. If you feel like your heart is beating out of your chest, that's how I learned my share size is too big. If I don't feel comfortable with this, I'm going to go and move it down. All of a sudden I'm very relaxed and I'm back in my trading zone. I'm not getting out early. You have to find out where your comfort level is in relation to your position size. Most people have no idea. That's what they need to learn: they need to learn it on paper. I had a guy who came in and he started just trading with 5,000 shares. I go, "What are you, nuts?" He said, "No. I have to make a certain amount of money." I'm like, "Who are you? I've been doing this 23 years and I'm not trading with 5,000 shares." First of all, it's so hard to get fill on 5,000-

Jane: In or out.

Stefanie: Yes, but he was like a cowboy. I'm like, "You don't even know what you're doing," and of course he lost and he went down to a 1,000. I'm like, "You're not even ready for a 1,000. You need to number one, paper trade. All right? Then, start small," and it took him so long to get to that point. A lot of people do that. They think that trading is gambling for them. Until you learn how to do it, you're gambling. Most people out there who are trading are gambling. They shouldn't be trading. It's a career. You know?

Jane: Definitely.

Stefanie: You have to learn and hone your craft, and you need experience. I always recommend four earning seasons to really master it. You need to go through it four times to really learn how these things trade. Earning season is the best for day trading. Oh. My God. Before and after I don't gamble into it, but before they're coming out, like the last 25 minutes, before they report, before four o'clock, those things go up, they go down, then I get out. They're amazing. That's it. Other than that it's very slow in between, then I'll swing trade. But I won't swing trade during earning season, because again, that's gambling. You don't know if they're going to miss, or another company in that sector is the worst. You asked what is the worst trade I've ever had, right?

Jane: Yeah. Your biggest loss.

Stefanie: Yeah. My biggest loss. Yeah. That was a very long time ago; obviously we learn when we're first starting. Right? I was swing trading, number one. I was swing trading at the firm.

Jane: Okay.

Stefanie: Onsite trading. I was in three semiconductor stocks. I was in AMAT, and I think it was LRCX, or MAXM, I forgot which ones they were, but it was three of them, and I was long. They all looked so good, it was a perfect setup, and it was definitely greedy to take all three. I learned the hard way to only take one stock in a sector because the next day, one of them was downgraded. They were all three of them down. Man, yeah. It was horrible. It was bad. I mean, look, on my worst day I lost $7,000.00. That was my worst in 23 years.

Jane: That's great.

Stefanie: It's not great, it's not bad. I had 500 shares back then, I was trading 500 share lots, but still they were all down a lot, like three, four points, whatever it was. My best day was much better than my worst day.

Jane: How big was your best day?

Stefanie: My best day, okay, it was 1996 or '97. A whole table was really bearish, and the market was really bad, it was down a couple hundred, and we were all putting on some shorts overnight, and one of my traders said, "You know, Stef, if we hit 500, the circuit breakers are going to go off and forget about it. Let's put it on. We're heading there." So we all started going in even heavier on the short side, and of course it happened. It was closed, they closed the market early, circuit breaker, and we're all sitting there going, Okay. We have nothing to do, we're short so much-

Jane: Yeah.

Stefanie: The next day they gapped it down and my account was up $50,000.00.

Jane: Wow.

Stefanie: But, okay, they opened it down, and then things went up so fast. I had a clerk, we're all yelling to the clerk to get us out at the same time. You cannot get out, it was different then. Now, you have one button you can push, and you're out of all of your positions. We didn't have that then. We're all yelling his name to buy this, buy that, so by the time I got out of everything I was up by $25,000.00. It was like you couldn't even get out fast enough. It was impossible. You know? Up and down so much. Right. That was my best day as far as an overnight trade. I have longer term trades that I've done extremely well on, but as far as a short-term, I was a swing trader back then. That was definitely one of my best days, but it was painful, because I could not get out. You know what? I learned a lesson. I have learned to get out, quick. That happened again, this past August, with that flash crash.

Jane: I wasn't really trading then.

Stefanie: Okay. In August we had a flash crash where we went down major, especially the one day. You learn, as a trader you definitely learn over time, but let's see, wait, let me just get the exact date it was really crazy, it was back-

Jane: That was before my daughter went to daycare.

Stefanie: August 21st, 2015, we crashed. We went from 203, wait, we went down to 182 in change, and then bounced all the way back up again. I learned, I got out into the crash instead of waiting. You definitely learn. I've learned so many things, and that's just experience. Right? A lot of people don't quite realize you need to experience it. Not just once, but you need to experience a pattern a few times, and then you become like a robot. That's really the key to trading, just trade robotically. There are things that happen, like something really bad happened, I remember when in Japan, they had that tsunami happen.

I'm programmed so that if there's something bad that comes across the tape, I immediately just short. I don't think about anything. I immediately put protection on if I have longs, of course, or just go short. Then, I contemplate, oh, my God, that's horrible, what happened? I'm robotically programmed to just hit that button. That's my job, like a policeman is programmed so that if they see somebody with a gun, he's going to shoot him. Ask questions afterwards. After 23 years I'm like okay, it's kind of, I don't know, kind of bad, but I'm programmed to just go short. Then I ponder what just happened afterwards. Yeah. No. This is the best job in the whole world. I get to be home with my kids.

Jane: Yeah. How do you balance the trading life with your kids?

Stefanie: Yeah. The market closes at four o'clock, but I'm definitely having my own business. I often work until 10, 11 o'clock at night. Doing business stuff. They're teenagers now, and I didn't work for many, many years so that I could stay home when they really needed me. When they were young, they couldn't do things for themselves. Now my kids are very self-sufficient and very independent, and I like that. I love that they can do things on their own. My daughter's driving right now, and she's going to college. It's different, now. I sacrificed many years, so that I could be there for them, and I'm very fortunate that I could do that. I know a lot of women cannot do that, but I feel like I made that sacrifice. I travel a lot now, and my daughter was like, "Oh. You weren't around, Mom, you travel a lot," and I'm like "Yeah. That's how I could pay for your prom dress. You know that really expensive prom dress that we just bought?" I would never have been able to buy that if I hadn't made that trip, so they understand. Teenagers are teenagers. Kids are kids. They remember the one thing that you couldn't do for them. Not the 50 things you did for them, just that one thing. They are like, "Mom, remember eight years ago when you couldn't do that, or you didn't do that?" I'm like, "Oh. My God."

Jane: I hear you.

Stefanie: They always blame the mother; they don't blame the father. It's the mother's fault. It's always the mother's fault. It's hard. I'll tell you, Jane, there's definitely a constant struggle. Women have it tougher, because we have to do it all.

Jane: Yeah. What do you think the biggest hurdles are for women to getting into trading?

Stefanie: I think it's really not a hurdle, because you can do it from home. I think the biggest hurdle for women is just that an outside job is really hard. I had a friend of mine who was a lawyer, and I felt so bad for her when our kids were in nursery school. She had three kids. She was constantly traveling to Canada, she was commuting, it was crazy for a while. I felt so bad, and I said, "Look. What can I do for you? Can I please help you? Let me drive your kids home. I'll do the play dates." She was so appreciative and I said, "I'm doing it anyway. My kids are having fun, and so let me help you." I felt so bad, but on the weekends she would take my kids. "No, it's the weekend, I'm home, let me take your kids." She would say to me, "Stefanie, how are you doing your job as a mother? I don't know how you're doing that." I'd say to her, "Brenda, how are you doing your job?"

Jane: Right.

Stefanie: You know? We really respected each other, because it's hard. Now, I'm doing both, obviously, but my kids are older. It's hard when they're younger, it really is, because there are things, there are recitals, you take a day off for this, there's a half day, you got to take it off, your baby is in childcare, but when they get to elementary school there are days off, there's this, they get sick. Right?

Yes. When they're sick, I would have been fired 100 times. If I had to work for somebody, I would have been fired, because there's always somebody sick and they cannot do it. Now, they're sick, I'm home, and everybody in my room knows, "Look, my kids come first. If I have to take them to the doctor, I cannot make the meeting. You guys are going to have to make deals until I get back." They're really cool about that. They come first; your kids always come first.

Jane: Definitely. Now, when you're traveling, do you still trade when you're on the road?

Stefanie: Oh, yeah. I was trading in Vegas at four o'clock in the morning.

Jane: Wow. I had swing trades when I was out there; I made a whole bunch of money in Vegas on swing trades.

Stefanie: So, sweet. Yeah. I actually did pretty good in Vegas. I was just there for the Money Show, so that was challenging, because I was waking up at four o'clock in the morning running my trading room. I have my laptop, my microphone, no matter where I am, I'm running it. That's the best part about this job. It's online, so I can do it anywhere. I was doing that, then trading, and then I was going down, because we had a booth there, to run at the convention.

I was doing that, and giving presentations, but then the market closes at one o'clock when you're on the West Coast, and of course there is stuff afterwards. I was staying up late. I was burning the candle at both ends; it was really hard. I was exhausted, but it was exciting. I'm always trading; I don't ever stop trading.

Jane: Very nice. Now, what's your home setup? Do you just have a laptop with monitors, or what do you have as your home setup?

Stefanie: I have three screens and a main computer that's not a laptop, it's hardwired. Then, I have a laptop with another screen, because a lot of times I'll be running a trading room, or I'll be doing the class in a different room, so I actually have two different things going on at one time, or I'll do coaching. I do one-on-one coaching. I really have three main screens, and of course a television that's just on, but muted. Really, three is good for me. Could I use three more? I could. I probably will get three more, very soon. It's like shoes-

Jane: Right.

Stefanie: You can never have enough products.

Jane: You always want more space to put things, more charts, or more information.

Stefanie: Yes. More stuff. I zone in on what I need to zone in on, so I have my futures, I have my charts, you get everything set up that you need, and that's it. I mean, how many things can you really watch at one time? Also, you don't want to be too spread out. I like to just zone in on what's really happening, the prints, wherever the volume is coming in, I zone in. I can watch a lot of stuff at one time, but there are a lot of people who don't have that ability. They cannot be in more than one stock, and they cannot concentrate, because they didn't map it out. Once you map it out, you know when you're getting in and when you're getting out. If it goes against you, you know where you're getting out. If it moves up, you don't even have to think about anything; you can move on to the next trade.

Jane: Yeah. There's confidence in your trade.

Stefanie: Right. Most people who get in, they don't know, so they have to watch that thing like a hawk. That's the problem. Now, hold on, I'm just going to actually scale out of a trade.

Jane: Yeah. No worries.

Stefanie: I'm actually trading while I'm doing this interview with you.

Jane: I cannot do that, because I would get myself in trouble. I have my screens in the background, very tiny, so I'm not doing that.

Stefanie: Okay. Only because I got into it before...I bought the, hold on, wait. It's an option trade. 169, so I bought the Apple calls, the 100 calls at $1.69 when it broke above that dark pool print. Now, I'm going to close them at, I mean, Apple might go up, but this market looks like it's going to go down. I'm closing them at $1.84; at $1.86 I got filled. Nice.

Jane: Very nice.

Stefanie: I made, yeah, 20 cents an option. Do you do options?

Jane: I told myself once I hit my $100,000 in profits goal, that I would start looking into options. It's just a threshold for myself, just to pass that, and then I'll start learning something else new.

Stefanie: Okay. Yeah. I only started doing options a year ago. I was always spooked out by them. How do you make money? There are so many ways you can lose. It does this, it does that, if you don't get it right, it's not as liquid - there are a lot of ways that you could lose money doing options. Number one, is you have to learn how to trade first, which is great. You're doing that, you're doing great. Once you're successful and you know where you're getting in and getting out, you can pick. It depends on what you trade, but Apple is great, great options on Apple. Great options on Facebook. Great options on the SPY. I'll do the VIX. There are certain things, then there's horrific options on things. You learn. What I love about it is I don't have to put so much money in.

Jane: That's what I've heard.

Stefanie: Yes. Again, I paper traded for six weeks before I did them. I stuck to my rules. I have a trader in my room, this girl Rickie, so my room is really female-dominated, I mean most of the people teaching in there are females, so Rickie teaches options. She came to me years ago, and she was an engineer, and she got into an accident, I think a motorcycle accident where she was unable to do her job and trading was all she had.

She didn't know how. She knew options, but she didn't know how to trade well. She needed help with that and I felt so bad for her. I said, "You know, Rickie, I'm going to do whatever I can to help you." I just felt like I needed to help this woman. I said, "You've got to make me a promise: once I teach you how to trade, you've got to teach me how to do options." I've sat in option meetings, and my head rotated like the Exorcist. No. Seriously, I couldn't understand, they lost me after 10 minutes, I was gone. I just zoned out. I just couldn't grasp it.

I spent years training Rickie, and Rickie was the best student. She listened, she repeated, she got everything, and then now, last year, she said, "Stefanie, I know you haven't been wanting to do options, but I'm going to teach you how to do them the way you trade." I couldn't do them the way she does them, but she knew how I traded. She said, "This is how you do them." I said, "Oh. My God." She said, "You know where the SPY is going, you call it out every day, you can trade it doing these options, and you're only going to need a couple hundred dollars, that's it. Instead of a couple hundred thousand." Because I'm trading my own money, now. I'm not trading firm money, like I was years ago.

Number one, I don't like to trade so much capital; I'd rather buy a house.

And, you only need to have a small trading account. You don't need to have that much money. She taught me options and it changed my life, Jane. I feel like I'm on a different level, now, like, wow, why didn't I do this earlier? I don't think I was ready to do it, earlier. You do it whenever you feel that you're ready, but you learn and paper trade. Rickie is amazing, so she teaches options in my room. She does a meeting every Tuesday, like an hour meeting, and she does coaching. I have another girl, Scooter, who runs my room when I'm not there, or if my screens were to go out.

Jane: Yeah.

Stefanie: In two seconds, she would take it over, and have block trades, everything. She takes the chat every day, and she makes it really nice. She puts everybody's charts in it, and she counts up all the dark pool prints, and she puts it together for the next day for everybody. They're amazing. I have so many amazing women in my room, as well. We've become friends. A lot of them are Canadians. They have a whole Canadian girls club going, now.

Jane: Very nice.

Stefanie: Yeah. It's definitely like family. There are a lot of great male traders too; in fact, my trader of the year was Wayne. We call him the cowboy. Everybody has nicknames in my room. He's the cowboy, and he's 72 years old. 72! and the trader of the year. He's phenomenal. He paper traded the longest. He was my longest paper trader. I would yell at him, and he'd be paper trading making money for a year. I was finally like, "Wayne, you got it. You can do it."

Jane: He followed the rule, though.

Stefanie: He did.

Jane: Four earning seasons.

Stefanie: He did. He really did; he wanted to prove to himself. All of a sudden, last year, around April he comes in the room, and he's like, "I'm not talking to you." He was angry with me, and I'm like, "What's the matter? What did I do wrong? Did I call out something that didn't work?" He goes, "I had to pay taxes this year, for the first time." We were all like, "Oh. My God. Why is he mad at me?" Finally, he spills it out. I'm like, "Oh. My God." Wow. Yeah. It was pretty funny, though, and he did really, really well this year, and now he teaches. He does presentations for the group. It's really great. I really give the ball to anybody who wants to do a presentation and teach a strategy. I give them control and they can do meetings after the market on Saturdays. A whole bunch of them go in the room and teach each other things. It's great. It's just good to have people around you.

Jane: What I really like, too, about having a trading room in the background is A, the audible; and B, the community; because trading behind the screen by yourself can be lonely. It's nice to have a room where you are a participant, so you feel like you are not necessarily alone.

Stefanie: Right. Yes. Support. It's really good support. You're learning, and that's the best part, too.

Jane: Besides the rules, and everything else we covered, what would you say to a new trader starting off, especially a new female trader?

Stefanie: Yeah. I think I pretty much said it. I mean, number one, female, non-female, I think right now that the females get huge respect in my room. I don't know what happens in other rooms, but my room, maybe because I'm running it, I don't know. I haven't been in other rooms, so I don't know, but in my room it's not gender at all. It's you're a trader; everybody's a trader. You're either a good trader, or not a great trader; some traders are better. We know who to follow and watch. Some of my traders are really, really good, but again, not every call they make is going to be great. Again, just by paper trading, you have to prove to yourself that your system works. No matter what system you're doing, you have to prove that it works. That's really key. Again, paper trade. I cannot stress that enough. People don't have the patience, but you need patience to trade.

Jane: You've got to learn the market before you just jump into it, I think.

Stefanie: Yes. You have to see things happen over and over again. You have to experience it all, but enjoy the process. Everyone is so antsy, oh, my God, "I've got to trade", the market is not going anywhere. It's always going to be here. It's the same patterns, pretty much, over and over again, and you just have to find which stocks are changing trends, up to down, down to up. The market goes in two directions. You make money going up, you make money going down. If you're only trading one way, you're cheating yourself, because there are plenty of great trades on both sides, but again, mapping it out is really key.

Jane: Definitely. Who do you use for trading platform and/ or charting information?

Stefanie: I use a lot of different companies. I wish that they made one software that did everything I needed. Really. I use DAS Trader Pro for my main software. It's just great charting, for me. It's just very friendly to me. They have a top 20 list which is great. In the morning it has dark pool data feeds, so I can see all of that volume when it comes in. They don't have a block trade indicator, so I have to use Charles Schwab Block Trader Indicator. Now, I use Lightspeed; it also has both. It's great. It also has a block trade indicator. They're the only two companies that have that. Lightspeed and Schwab. I also use the Trade Exchange for News; I have it up on my screen all day. They're just a great news service. I use TC2000 for scanning. I use thinkorswim for futures. I use Livevol Pro, which is new. I just started using that, which is great. I use Trade Ideas for unusual options activity.

Jane: I use them, too.

Stefanie: You do? Yeah. They're good. I mean, it's just a question of what you feel comfortable with. Everybody has their own that they really like better than others. You have to have that dark pool data feed.

Jane: If you were asked to recommend three books, or DVDs, or learning tools for new traders, what would those be, besides *Reminiscences of a Stock Operator*?

Stefanie: I'd recommend my workshops on my website. They are really good. I do have a good series called Counting the Cards of Wall Street. I have a lot of introductory workshops about how to read the tape. Trader on the dark pool. Each one of my workshops really has a correction, that I personally spot, and I've personally taken pictures before it happened. I have all my tweets there where I'm telling you it's bearish, here are the prints, you see the pictures of them. I'll be honest, I've captured the last 10 corrections in workshops. You know? I don't know anybody else who did that. They haven't come forward, but I've actually captured all the dark pool trades. If you really want to learn, that's a great place. *Reminiscences of a Stock Operator* by Edwin Lefèvre and Roger Lowenstein . That is my favorite. I've read a lot of books, but nothing hit me the way that book hit me. I mean, that was just the best one. I've heard *Trading Beyond the Matrix* by Van Tharp is good. I haven't read it, yet. I have it on my desk. I just haven't read it yet, but my traders have raved about it. Books are books, but I really think you need to experience the market. I think that the most important part is to actually experience, and learn from those experiences.

Jane: If people want to follow you, what are your social media handles, like on Twitter, and StockTwits?

Stefanie: Okay. On Twitter, Larry Berman gave me the nickname volumeprintcess. You can find me there. On StockTwits, I'm very, very popular. I think I just hit 23,000 people: the_stock_whisperer. You can follow me there. I really do put out a ton of content every day. For example, today I took pictures of those Apple prints and posted them up there. Any time there are dark pool prints on the SPY, I take pictures and post them out there. Those are my two main sites where I'm constantly pushing content out, every day.

Jane: Very nice. I just actually started following you on Twitter, myself.

Stefanie: Okay. Are you on StockTwits?

Jane: I'm not on StockTwits.

Stefanie: You should go on there. It's great. You can follow traders, stocks, or both. You know? I love it. I mean, I just find a lot of traders; I help a lot of traders. For me, I'll be honest, Jane, I feel like this is my calling. You know? To help people. My mother always told me I should be a teacher, and I said, "No, Mom. I really love the market." Here I am; I'm doing both. For me, there are so many traders out there who have no idea what they're doing. To help people is priceless.

Jane: Definitely.

Stefanie: It's a good way to give back.

Jane: It's very satisfying to know that you've helped somebody to become self-sufficient.

Stefanie: Yes. Money is money. I'll be honest: you know, Jane, you make money, lose money, make money. It's great. I have money. I have enough money to put my daughter through four years of college, medical school. My son, through college. I'm good, but money is money, and there are other things in life which are more important than money. Number one is health. Health is really important. Number two is helping people. Helping others. It's priceless. Every day that I help somebody or teach them, and help them to help their families, and feed their families, is just a great day for me. It definitely goes beyond just trading. Trading is just trading - okay, wow, great. Somebody once said that to me years ago. They go, "Trading is so selfish. It's a selfish career." I said, "Well, I don't think of it that way," because I'm making money, and I'm putting food on the table for my kids. You cannot say that's selfish. I'm providing a roof over their heads. I'm like, "Okay." You're just pushing a couple of buttons, buying and selling, but to help others, yeah, it's a whole other dimension. You know, you're doing this to help others.

Jane: That's the whole reason for the book. Exactly. To help others.

Stefanie: It's so great.

Jane: I have one more question, sorry it just popped into my head, but-

Stefanie: Sure.

Jane: I don't know what your husband does, but how does he deal with your success as a successful female trader?

Stefanie: I'm divorced.

Jane: Okay.

Stefanie: He had issues with me being financially independent. We'll just leave it at that.

Jane: Yeah. For sure. Everybody has their different egos, and different scenarios, it goes back to-

Stefanie: Exactly. Yeah.

Jane: The psychology of trading. You know? Sometimes it's difficult for your friends and your family to realize that you're becoming successful in trading. I mean, I know a lot of people who are asking, "Why go into trading? You're crazy. It's a gamble." Then, you start becoming successful and then they-

Stefanie: Right.

Jane: They can become resentful. For sure.

Stefanie: Right. He told me I should get a real job. Yeah. It's a great feeling to be able to support yourself, independently. It's great. Doing what you love, no matter what it is. If you're doing what you love, and you can support yourself and your family, as a woman, it's incredible. An incredible feeling. There are always going to be people out there who are going to be envious, because they're not doing that. You know? They wish they had that passion, because you're doing what you love. Don't you love trading every day?

Jane: I love it. My husband sees it, and actually my husband's the one who reminded me that I used to be a value trader long-term. I had an amazing investment, and he said, "You have a natural talent for this, you need to look at it." I just started studying, and it took me maybe nine months before I started really paper trading, and then from there it just grew. It's great to have someone be a good supporter, to be thankful for my talent, and to see and tell me, too, that I'm just happier. I love my job now. Coming down, and sitting down at my desk - I love it, and I look forward to it every day.

Stefanie: Me, too. I'm so excited every day, the market's open. Oh, my God, what's going to happen? What am I going to trade? Love it. I don't know what else would feel like that. Working for somebody else, no. Getting in your car and getting stuck in traffic somewhere, horrible. Nobody's going to pay you what you can pay yourself.

Jane: Yeah.

Stefanie: Yeah. I love it.

Jane: Very nice. I think we've covered everything that I wanted to cover. Is there anything else?

Stefanie: I do a lot of free webinars, teaching. It's all good. The more people that I can teach and help, the better off, because it's us against the big guys, it's not us against each other. You know? Everybody thinks, oh, my God, why do you share your secrets, why do you do that? I'm like, "Just because I share my secrets, I can still trade the way I do and still have the same profits. It's not going to take away from my profits. I'm going to help you." There are a lot of people out there that are not as nice as we are.

Jane: Definitely. I don't know if you know *The Secret*, but to me, the stock market is truly the abundance where everybody can win, because people can win on the long, and people can win on the short.

Stefanie: Right.

Jane: It's a win-win for everybody, if you know what you're doing.

Stefanie: Exactly. Yeah.

Stephanie Clark Burke

USA

Twitter: @Wallstreetsteph
Gmail: Wallstreetsteph@gmail.com
Facebook: Stephanie Clark Burke

I first met Stephanie out in Carlsbad, California. We were both asked to speak in a seminar to empower women about trading sponsored by Trade Ideas. We met and quickly discovered we are very similar in personalities. Stephanie B., like Stefanie K., was trading back in the 1990s before home internet was easily accessible and is looking to bring day trading back into her life again.

Jane: What really made you interested in trading? And when did you start? What was the story that brought you to trading?

Steph: I started in November of '92 as an employee for Block Trading, not really knowing anything about stocks. I was in charge of helping the customers open their accounts and watching them trade. I would also monitor their trades. I saw the kind of money that could be made.

Jane: So you were more on the administrative side versus the actively trading side?

Steph: I was for three years. So what lured me to trading? Seeing the money that was being made. No doubt.

Jane: And then what was the push to make you go into trading? I mean, you saw the money being made, but how did you transition into trading from just being on the administrative side?

Steph: I decided to take the plunge and quit my job, and I had someone willing to put up money for me who believed in me as well. I guess I really got pretty lucky on that. By trading her money for one month, I mean my first month, I was up $26,000 on $80,000.

Jane: That's amazing. Great returns.

Steph: Yes, and at that point, I wanted more money to use for trading. So I approached some other friends of mine to double that money. They gave me $160,000.

Jane: For trading capital?

Steph: Yes.

Jane: And out of curiosity, when they gave you the capital, did they ask for any sort of return on it?

Steph: Yeah, I was paying them a split of 60/40, or 65/35 ... 65/35.

Jane: So they were getting 65% of profits?

Steph: No, I was getting 65%.

Jane: Yeah, I was going say, that's not really a winning ratio.

Steph: The first account I traded 50/50 profits, but after the first month, knew I was on it. Not a doubt in mind that I got this.

Jane: Back then, it was very different trading than it is today, right? Because you were on the floor of the trading room, right, at Block Trading?

Steph: At Block Trading they had little pods set up, four customers to a pod, with one person to input your trades. And, the spreads were larger. We traded in fractions. Eighths, quarters, were mostly what we were looking for. I mean, anything over three eighths and more, you were banging bucks.

Jane: And I know you mentioned before on your interview with Trade Ideas that every trade was 1,000 shares, right? No matter what, you were just buying 1,000 shares.

Steph: Yes, everything was 1,000 shares. And a block trade is 1,000 shares, or more. You could have done 500, but it was the same commission for 500 or 1000 at that time. I guess the last time I traded was 2007, 2008.

Jane: Very different from back in the 90s.

Steph: Yeah.

Jane: Now, when you first got interested, did you have someone who you really worked with at Block that helped you once you transitioned into your trading job? Or had you learned from the experience of being around everybody?

Steph: No, I think because I had enough experience just watching others and being around it in the office, I had a comfort level that other new people coming in didn't possess. I also think it was an advantage to me that I didn't know a lot about the industry. I wasn't as technical, because I was more of a trend trader. I was watching more of a sector. I was dealing with what things were moving more on a daily basis and a weekly basis than long term.

Jane: So you were trading more the charts, right?

Steph: Yeah, well, really just what the stocks were doing, what was moving that day, what sector was moving, and whether it was tech or bio or pharmaceuticals. That's what I was trading that day, what was moving.

Jane: At that time how did you guys get that information?

Steph: A lot of times I did not watch any charts. It was more based on the trends of my clients.

Jane: Got it. It can be a lot easier to go with momentum instead of against it, because when that momentum does flip, man, you better watch out.

Steph: Right, and I'm not going to try to prove it wrong. That is another reason why I think that female traders don't have that ego. Female traders have more humility than the men in the industry.

Jane: How were you gaining this information? Because the internet was not as accessible as it is today.

Steph: We had someone calling out news, like Associated Press (AP), and we would read Bloomberg. We would read the wire, we had CNBC on 24/7, and you know, a lot of stuff was trading on news and just scalping. You know, scalping was the deal back then. Yeah, that's why

I did so many trades, because I could actually put in a bid at the bid price and sometimes get filled under the offer. I'd just do a trade in between the spread of the bid and the ask and bank.

Jane: Nice.

Steph: Yeah, whatever the offer was, I was always just below it, even if it was a penny below it.

Jane: Great strategy.

Steph: So I was always getting executed faster than most people.

Jane: Yeah. So how many trades would you say you were executing in a day at that time?

Steph: I would say, even when I first started out, I was doing 30 round trips a day. And then, you know, at my peak, it averaged about 400, you know, 350,000 to 400,000 shares.

Jane: Wow.

Steph: Yeah.

Jane: When you were there, what sort of setup was it? Obviously it was different in the 90s because technology wasn't the same.

Steph: We had level 2s, and we had Instinet, which I don't even know if that's around anymore. I don't think so. We could see block trades on Instinet, like institutional trading. And if there were sides, you know, on bid or offer, we knew what was going to drive something up or hold it. If there was a block of, you know, 500,000 shares sitting on Microsoft, it was going take a little while to spit that out. When we would see that offer eaten up, we'd know it was going to keep moving.

Jane: Exactly. If you saw there was a big giant purchase, say at 9.50, you knew that was pretty much going to become a good support level.

Steph: Yes.

Jane: Now, when you started trading, did you do any sort of research or read any books, or anything like that, or it was just pure experience that you went on?

Steph: No, nothing. Everything was more instinctual based on me watching those stocks on a daily basis. I would trade the same stocks every day, pretty much. I may have added one or two or three new ones, but for the most part I traded Microsoft and Intel every day.

Jane: At that point in time, it wasn't options, it was strictly the equities, correct?

Steph: Yes, no options. There were people doing that, but I didn't. And there were some people trading them in New York, but I didn't.

Jane: Your office was based out of Texas, right? It was based out of Houston?

Steph: Yes, out of the Galleria. We were at Galleria in the Galleria Financial Mall.

Jane: Out of curiosity, how many people were in the office at the time? And were you the only woman in the office trading?

Steph: There was one other woman out of probably 65 traders and there were 15 or 20 other employees. We even had a runner so that we never had to leave our desks. They'd go get us breakfast, lunch, do our errands, whatever we needed.

Jane: You were tied to your desk at that time. It was not, hey, I'm going to trade from my laptop from the beach, like you see some people advertising now.

Steph: No. Sometimes I would be in a couple of positions where I'd really be in the money, and I could run home and go to the gym.

Jane: When you did that, were there any software tools, or anything that you used?

Steph: No, there was nothing. I had an assistant who would input the trades, and they would call me. I would bonus them out, depending on how much I made that month.

Jane: When you were setting up for your day, what did you do back then? How did you prep for your day? Did you sit down at your desk and just trade what was active?

Steph: I would pull up charts from the day before, so that I could see what they were doing. Maybe the day before, maybe the past week, but not a lot. Just seeing what trend of the futures and the Dow were doing.

Jane: Got it. How often did you swing a position overnight?

Steph: Not very often. A couple of times a month. In the beginning, in the first year, never. In the second year, you know, I just started taking a little more risk, but I would only do it if I was in the money, and you know, the one time that I did it out of the money, I got burned royally. I'm talking about CMRC, which I'll never forget. An expensive margarita.

Jane: Yes, the margarita trade. Now, with your trading at that point in time, if it went against you, did you add to your positions?

Steph: I would sometimes, if I really thought it was going to come back. A lot of what I did was just trusting my gut.

Jane: OK.

Steph: There really wasn't much strategy, other than wishful thinking.

Jane: Nowadays for news sources, it's very different. You have Twitter. You've got all this social media, Stock Twits, and more.

Steph: Right, there's so much more information.

Jane: Now you have instantaneous news. I know that you're coming back to trading. How do you see the price action today in comparison to when you were trading before? Do you think it's more volatile based on the news that's accessible?

Steph: I think it's going to be easier, actually, but I think I'm going to be holding things a lot longer, and I might be trading more than 1,000 shares at a time. But when I start again I'm going to be trading smaller positions, maybe 500 shares and get into maybe one or two positions.

Jane: Yes.

Steph: I'm really studying the charts now. Which I never did before. That goes also for all my trader friends from the past. I've talked to two other guys who are getting back into it that I used to trade with in '98. They've just come back, and they are doing the same thing. I just talked to them about the software. Everyone is into the chart patterns now.

Jane: Well, you can start to see trends and patterns. Everybody is studying those same patterns. When people have the software and they know how to alert themselves of these stocks that set up certain patterns, then they become the momentum stocks. Today I'm watching SGY, which has gone from $7.00 up to $9.50. That is 36 percent gain in one day. And seeing that, you can see that people are finding out about these stocks and the volume just explodes.

Steph: Right, because more people start watching and more people start trading it.

Jane: Exactly.

Steph: The volume is going to go up.

Jane: So, you can see that happen. I'm curious to know how different your perspective is based on when you were trading before. It seems like everybody had the same news sources back then, and now everybody has the same news sources as well at their fingertips, but now the reaction can be instantaneous, instead of a delay of minutes or half an hour as when you were trading with Block Trading.

Steph: I'm interested in how the executions are going to go for me. That's going to be the tough one for me to swallow, because I'm used to having immediate executions. Especially when I was getting out of a position if it was moving. You know, if I was buying I would put in an offer a half over the bid and get filled. That was how the software was designed for the executions.

Jane: That's something that I try to tell people about getting into trading. It's not just the learning curve of the market, which you already have, but it's learning all the technology and software. It's all the extra stuff that you have to learn as well. If you're learning how to run Excel spreadsheet, you have to learn how it works before you can put in all the information and run the equations to get everything out the way you want. Same thing with trading platform software. You have to practice. And with your trades at Block Trading, were you trading multiple different stocks at once, or were you just in Intel and that's what you were trading for the day?

Steph: Oh no, I was in multiple stocks at once. When the whole trend was really moving, I mean if I was in the tech stocks, I would get in all of them.

Jane: Ok.

Steph: If I was in Intel, I was normally in Microsoft and Cisco. If there was a big move in the market, I was in all of them for that sector. They would usually, but not always, move all together. If one wasn't, and I had bought it, I would just try to get out flat. If I realized I was making a mistake entering in a stock, flat was my friend. A flat trade was a winner when the stock was going against me.

Jane: Well, you can have a good trade if you get out and it continues to tank. That's a good trade.

Steph: Yes; let the winners run and cut my losses on everything else.

Jane: Great habits. And as far as your risk management, which you touched on a little bit, did you have a certain amount that you were willing to lose percentage wise, or dollar amount wise, for the day, or per trade?

Steph: I think back then I tried not to lose more than a quarter point. It also depended on what stock it was. For the bigger spread stocks, I was willing to possibly risk a little more. I think it all depended maybe on how much I profited for the month. There were several aspects that played in the factor of how much risk, but I don't think there was a set amount. Maybe a quarter loss my way, you know, $250, $300 was like the average. And that's on 1,000 shares.

Jane: When you were trading, did you have the ability to put in stops, or was it strictly in and out, and you just had to monitor each trade?

Steph: I had to monitor each trade. I had two monitors with say twelve stock quote screens of level two, and maybe a couple of charts that I could pull up on each individual. The screens at the top were Instinet and our execution screens. It wasn't even all on the same page for the first few years.

Jane: Ok.

Steph: We're talking old school. I was writing all my trades down. At the end of the day, I had to compare the trades they had put in my accounts to my trades and make sure there were no trades that somebody else had executed. I had to reconcile my account every afternoon.

Jane: Right, because you had one person that dealt with four people's trades, correct?

Steph: Correct.

Jane: So you were using mental stops, or getting out at break even.

Steph: Yes.

Jane: Now, what was the biggest loss that you had?

Steph: Yeah, $256,000 short 3,000 shares of CMRC.

Jane: Wow.

Steph: I don't even know what the heck it was back then, because GM had announced they were buying them. I forgot what it closed at when I left the office. The next morning it opened it up $50 from close. So I walked in down 150K, and it took me another 100K to get out. It was still climbing up on the open when I got out. Then it came back down, but not all the way back to where I opened my short. But I just took my losses. I wanted to throw up. And then I got angry. Because I broke the cardinal rule. Don't hold overnight out of the money, and especially not 3,000 shares. I mean, that was just idiotic.

Jane: What was the price of the stock at that time?

Steph: It was up there, $80 or something. Yeah, it was up there.

Jane: And what made you leave the office early that day?

Steph: I wanted to go meet a girlfriend for margaritas at Escalante's. We each had three margaritas.

Jane: And then you came back the next day.

Steph: Yes. I'd heard that the stock announced a GMC buyout and knew I was in trouble.

Jane: Ouch.

Jane: How did you recover from that?

Steph: Licked my wounds and kept on going. I did not let it faze me.

Jane: Did you take any time off from trading?

Steph: No, I just wanted to hurry up and make that money back. I backed it up with my two biggest days ever.

Jane: Do you remember the stocks that you traded then and your biggest win on the flip side?

Steph: Well, I started trading CMRC, even after it burned me. After they announced the buyout, it ran up another 40 points, and then it dumped.

Jane: Yes, we see that happen nowadays, too.

Steph: Yeah, right. I mean, by the time the news normally hits the media ... Sell on news, buy on rumors, sell on news, which was almost the way back then. You know, we were like, shoot, by the time, it hit the sandy seas, it's almost time to do the opposite of what you think the stock's going to do.

Jane: Which you can definitely see with stocks today as well. With the news alerting services.

Steph: Totally.

Jane: They make the rumors, and then, it's boom, ok, it spikes up. Well now, it's time for a flip reversal move, because everybody's reacting, and it's going sell off.

Steph: I mean, there's so much insider trading that isn't ever talked about. People announce these news stories with intention to unload, you know, is my thought.

Jane: Well, the pump and dump...

Steph: A classic example is Enron completely going out of business, and all the top execs are selling. You know, you can look at that stuff. If you're watching a company go up, and they're selling off, and all the insiders from the company, get ready. That's another source of news: insider activity.

Jane: You can see that now with the big hedge fund investors such as Soros and Icahn. When a stock drops 20 percent, the big mutual funds and big houses typically can't hold it anymore. So you will see it sell off immediately, and then there's a bounce where you have other investors coming in, other big money coming in, and they buy it at a discount.

Steph: Back in the tech bubble there were so many short squeezes that were running things up, too. You know, stocks that have a huge short position is another source.

Jane: Yeah, you definitely see a lot of that now, a lot of short squeezes nowadays. And, now with your trading, where do you stand in coming back to trading?

Steph: I'm waiting on equity. You know, and basically, I'm going to be starting with $20,000, $25,000.

Jane: Yeah, coming back into it, it'll be easier if you start with $25,000, so you're outside the PDT rule.

Steph: Yeah. Right. Do they multiply your buying power based on equity?

Jane: In a margin account, yes. However, if you drop below the $25,000 for the PDT, then they will basically put you under the PDT rule, so then it's only three round trips in a rolling week instead of in a day. You can swing, but you are not allowed to intraday trade.

Steph: Right. I can't have that.

Jane: Yes, it will make it more difficult. When you were trading, did you really watch the level 2 at that time?

Steph: I did. Yeah, because you could see the blocks trades, and you could see which firms were trading the stock. If Goldman was trading it one way or another, and he's a major player, that made a factor in our eyes. You know, JP Morgan and Bear Stearns were big players back in the day.

Jane: When you were trading back then, do you think you had any barriers as a female in the trading world?

Steph: Definitely. I just don't think I was taken as seriously at all. I was only taken seriously by the people who really knew me that I was making money. I mean, people just did not believe that I was making money. And being blonde, I'm supposed to be a bimbo.

Jane: How did you compare profit wise to the men in your trading room?

Steph: I was always in the top three in our office, if not the top two.

Jane: I know you ended up trading from home later once your daughter was born. How was that? I mean, you had to bring in special lines because of internet speeds, right?

Steph: I had a T1 line in my house, which at the time was like $1,600 a month. I had a harder time trading because I was on speaker phone with everybody in the office. It was harder to have the energy and the camaraderie of everybody shouting at each other. We worked as a team and we had more eyes on more stuff. So, I could see a trading floor coming back.

Jane: Do you think there was more group mentality on the trading floor?

Steph: Yes, absolutely. People were yelling out what was moving, or watch the futures! There was more knowledge and there were more minds watching together.

Jane: Got it.

Steph: And if somebody was arguing a trade that was winning, it was also to their benefit to get everybody else in.

Jane: Right, of course.

Steph: Yeah.

Jane: You've done some exploring with Trade Ideas and checked out their free trading room. Have you seen how these stocks react after they've been talked about in the room? Sort of the same kind of idea as a trading floor without having to be there in person?

Steph: Yes. I have. It is a good place for people to learn.

Jane: And get to see software in action for free.

Steph: They get to try the software for free. So a huge positive to the room is that they can go in there every day and learn for free.

Jane: Anything else that you want to add about how different it was when you were trading in the 90s?

Steph: I think that the trading back then was much more intense. I mean I literally went into the office so excited and pumped up every day that I used to say I was playing the Super Bowl every day, plus the regular season. All the guys around me would say, "You have balls of steel." It was just so crazy.

Jane: What do you think the biggest hurdles are for females nowadays becoming day traders?

Steph: God, I mean it's still a male-dominated industry. Getting the money to trade I think is probably the biggest hurdle that I'm even having in coming back. I just don't want the pressure of trading someone else's money. I want to wait till I get my own money.

Jane: I feel the capital is a struggle for anybody getting into trading. Finding the trading capital, especially if they're working a nine to five job and bouncing from paycheck to paycheck.

Steph: I don't think there is any difference between men and women trading, personally. I think women are more gifted in trading. We are better multi-taskers. It's a proven fact. I mean I operate at a better function when I'm busy.

Jane: I agree we tend to be more focused.

Steph: And prioritize and keep the ego out of trade.

Jane: Do you think there is any issue with women having the confidence in getting into day trading? Or is trading out of their comfort zone?

Steph: Yeah, because that's the ego. I think that the male ego is so much stronger than a woman's. It's that self-doubt and self-fear that most women are plagued with for no reason whatsoever. It goes to the whole stereotype of what women are supposed to be in life. We're not supposed to be strong. It's a stereotype of what a woman still lives today. It's changing slowly, but that stigma of where a woman's place is as far as being a homemaker is still there.

Jane: Definitely.

Steph: We're supposed to be at home. I mean, I just got done dating a guy that, you know he said, "A woman is supposed to be home." I'm like, "Well honey, I ain't never going to be home."

Jane: So it's just not going to work.

Steph: "You got the wrong girl."

Jane: That's why you're done dating him, because he didn't let you be your true self.

Steph: Yeah, that lasted a month.

Jane: Very cool. I agree with you on the stereotype aspect. I feel like that's why many women don't even try it because they don't think they have the ability. When in reality, it's just a mental hurdle.

Seph: Right, yep.

Jane: When you were trading, how did you balance your trading life and your home life? I know obviously when you were at the firm, at Block Trading, you were there every day. Then once you got pregnant, did you find that the pregnancy affected your trading at all?

Steph: No, even when I was pregnant, I was fearless. Having to go to the bathroom and break away when I was in trade, that's when I had to quit. I definitely had to find balance and sticking with my rules, my trading rules that I would have, even on a daily basis for what my goals were, my trade goals. I had to stick with those.

Jane: What were those rules that you had? I don't think we've touched on them.

Steph: That really would just depend on what was happening every day. It really was about what the market was doing that day. On slow, dead days, I tried to take off and catch up. I mean in flat markets, I'm out. I would literally trade the first hour and get out and go catch up. On days where we were looking at volatility you just couldn't leave. You knew that week was just going to be busy at work.

Jane: Once you had the T1 high speed internet line at home, were you trading with your daughter?

Steph: No, because I had a live-in maid.

Jane: So you had help at the time.

Steph: Yes, I was making so much money, it didn't matter.

Jane: You had help to facilitate the trading aspect with a child at home.

Steph: Absolutely, because you could trade during the first couple hours of the morning. Then go about your day, come back, and trade the last 90 minutes.

Jane: Yeah, that's what I found, too.

Steph: I mean, I worked out. I had a trainer at 11:30 every day for an hour and a half. I would go work out and come back at lunch. I never traded during lunch. Not never, but for the most part, I had a pretty set schedule.

Jane: Was that when you were more at home once your daughter was born, or was that at the time you were at Block Trading?

Steph: Yeah, that was at Block Trading, because we were in a mall in the financial center. It was hooked to a country club right there.

Jane: At that time, there wasn't an ability to travel in trade, correct? You were either trading at Block Trading when you were there in the office or you were trading at home with your T1 line.

Steph: Well, no. When the Block Trading offices started opening, they would put me up in a hotel and pay for me to let their people, who were starting new accounts, sit behind me and watch how and what I traded. For that, they would pay to fly me out there and trade in some of their offices.

Jane: So you were training other people to trade with Block Trader before your daughter was born?

Steph: Yes. That was going on in '96, '97, '98. Then Block Trading went out of biz in '98. Right after we got married.

Jane: When did you have your daughter?

Steph: January of 2001.

Jane: What did you do between '98 and 2001? Before you were trading at home?

Steph: I traded with another company called Momentum Security. That's when I got interviewed on ABC News with Peter Jennings about women investing. I had my Trump interview and all that kind of stuff.

Jane: When you were at Momentum, were you also training others to trade at the time?

Steph: No, and I was the only girl. It was all guys. The girls were mostly in the administrative staff.

Jane: Was it like a prop firm, or you were just trading your own capital within that group?

Steph: At that point, I was trading my own capital. There were some guys that kind of broke away from Block Trading in the building process of Block. Our computer guys went and started their own company: Momentum Trading. I basically went to work for the competitor. Oh, they loved it when I came over.

Jane: Yeah, they knew you were a star at that time and you had the momentum going for yourself.

Steph: They all hated Chris Block. He was such an egomaniac. Everybody was okay with my now ex, but there was a lot of rivalry and bullshit. It was pretty humbling for me to go there and trade.

Jane: At the same time, you did really well when you were at Momentum Trading, correct?

Steph: I did do really well. I did very well. 2000 was my biggest year making over a million dollars.

Jane: How long did it take you before you felt successful in your trading career, after switching from being an administrator to trading on your own?

Steph: I knew right off the bat. I really just had a gut instinct that I got this, man. I am going to crush it. I just knew it.

Jane: That's great!

Steph: I mean you either feel it, or you don't. If I could have taught others how to do it better, I would be one rich lady. There's a lot of instinct factor I think there. Type A women, like you and I.

Jane: Yeah, and I believe as an administrator, you were watching the market and seeing the patterns and seeing how others were trading, so you were really learning in the process and seeing their trial and error.

Steph: Right.

Jane: Without actually having a direct mentor or someone guiding you, you learned through seeing others' pitfalls and gains.

Steph: Totally. Yes, and in my own mind, I was kind of thinking that client should've got out. He was being stubborn. He was not taking his loss and cutting it. Now he was doubling down and really messing up. You know? Of course, I wasn't talking about all that, but I was thinking in my own mind: I would've gotten out. I think that paper trading really helps.

Jane: Now, when you were looking for capital, were you practicing with paper trading with the newer market, the speed of the internet, Twitter, and instantaneous news?

Steph: I was for a little bit, but right now, with all this real estate stuff, I haven't had time. I mean I'm looking at closing 100 to 125 grand here soon.

Jane: Very nice. That's for your commission?

Steph: Yeah.

Jane: That's amazing. That means you'll have capital to jump back into trading!

Steph: Yes ma'am, that's what I'm talking about.

Jane: Very nice. Is there anything else that you would want to say to a newer trader, whether it's a man or a woman, who is coming into the trading world today?

Steph: I mean it mostly would be like if you have a passion for this, you've got to give it a try. If you're careful, than this isn't your gig. You're not ready for the Super Bowl. I do feel like it's got to be somebody who is strong-willed, courageous, and not afraid of failure. Failure can be success as well.

Jane: Yes.

Steph: Learning from our mistakes is our greatest gift.

Jane: Definitely, and that's it. You have to learn to be able to change it and see what went wrong to be able to stop it from happening in the future.

Steph: Right. Experience.

Jane: Yes, and that's what I always tell people, too. If you wanted to go be a surgeon, you're not just going to go to your friend, "Hey, I'm going to operate on you tomorrow." It's the same with jumping in the market. You can't just expect to be a pro overnight because others have had success. You need the time to study and learn the market.

Steph: Yep.

Jane: Wonderful. Well thank you, Steph. I look forward to hearing more about your return to trading

Steph: Okay, awesome. I'm happy to share. Have a great day.

Jane: Thanks, you too. Bye.

Steph: Bye.

Afterword

Through all of these interviews with various traders, you can see that it makes no difference what your background is that brings you to trading, or whether you are male or female. The bottom line is with dedication, hard work, and perseverance, you can succeed.

All the women in this book have a true passion for trading. That passion leads to their devotion to learn everything they need to learn in order to be profitable traders. You can see through their experiences that success did not happen for them overnight. Trading as a profession is not a get-rich-quick scheme. The traders here have experience extending from five months to over 25 years.

Know that they gave their time to help you learn, and for that, I'm thankful. With fewer females out in the public eye, it has been challenging to find women who are willing to share their trading biographies. So please thank these ladies for all the knowledge you have taken from their contributions.

You must learn an ocean of information in order to become profitable. You will have tough days in terms of losses and mental struggles, but know that this is part of the learning process. Try to follow the path that makes you feel most comfortable, and stay true to yourself.

If you are committed to leaving that nine to five job, put forth the effort every day. It is time to stop working. Stop making others rich. You can be like Jordan, and travel the world trading; or be like LaToya and Justine, working from home to be with their families. If you truly have that goal of breaking free from the daily grind, then start today!

Each day or night you set aside 30 minutes, one hour, or more to learn the market, you are on your way to your destination of financial freedom. The only person you have to let down is who you see in the mirror, so make yourself proud. Do the work and be kind to yourself in the process.

With these numbers it is easier than you think to make a six-figure salary from home.

50 weeks x 5 days a week = 250 days

$100,000/250 days = $400 a day in profits on average.

Go and make those profits happen! Live each day like it is your last! Carpe Profit!

Free Trading Tools

<u>Charting</u>
Trading View - bit.ly/Tview

<u>Scanning</u>
Finviz - bit.ly/FNVIZ

<u>Trading Room</u>
Trade Ideas - bit.ly/TIRoom

<u>Paper Trading</u>
Think or Swim - bit.ly/TOSPaper
Trading View - bit.ly/Tview

<u>Trading Platforms</u>
Ninja Trader - bit.ly/NTrader
Robinhood - bit.ly/Rhood

<u>Trading Analysis</u>
Profit.ly - bit.ly/tradeanalysis

Some of these bit.ly links are connected to affiliate pages if you choose to go with a paid service.

Books Recommended by the Traders Interviewed

An American Hedge Fund by Timothy Sykes

Market Wizards by Jack Schwager

Momo Traders by Brady Dahl

New Earth by Eckhart Tolle

Living in the Now by Eckhart Tolle

How You Can Trade Like a Pro by Sarah Potter

Drive by Daniel H. Pink

Mindset by Carol S. Dweck Potter

Trading in the Zone: Master the Market with Confidence, Discipline and a Winning Attitude by Mark Douglas

How to Profit in Bull and Bear Markets by Stan Weinstein

Trade Your Way to Financial Freedom by Van Tharp

Trading Beyond the Matrix by Van Tharp

Rich Dad Poor Dad by Robert T. Kiyosaki

The Big Leap: Conquer Your Hidden Fear and Take Life to the Next Level by Gay Hendricks

Reminiscences of a Stock Operator by Edwin Lefèvre and Roger Lowenstein

Smart Trading Plans by Justine Pollard

Recommended YouTube Channels

Airplane Jane

Travellight

Virtual Summit Media, LLC

Timothy Sykes

She CanTrade

The Stock Whisperer @ The Java Pit

CFD Trading & Share Trading Courses by Justine Pollard

About the Author

Jane Gallina AKA "Airplane Jane" started her career in February 2015 and has taken the day trading community by storm. As a loving wife and mother of two, Jane was seeking control of her financial future while remaining present for her young daughters. As a day trader, Jane has been able to accomplish that dream; quickly becoming one of the most successful female day traders under mentor Timothy Sykes. Through her blog, YouTube videos, and seminars Jane hopes to inspire and empower more individuals to break out of their comfort zone and try day trading. She believes in giving back to others we all become prosperous.